Well2Serve

by

Ken Hemphill

Auxano Press

Auxano
PRESS

Tigerville, South Carolina

ISBN 978-1497461918

Published by Auxano Press
Tigerville, South Carolina
www.AuxanoPress.com

Printed by Faith Printing Company
Taylors, South Carolina
www.FaithPrintingCompany.com

Dedicated to
Robert Meredith Edward Oswald IV (Ward)
My grandson
An active young man, who lives with a song on his lips
and love in his heart.
I pray that you will
grow in body, soul, and spirit
and give your life in service.

Contents

Acknowledgements vii

Introduction ix

1 Uniquely Created for Kingdom Service....................1

2 The Two Great Commandments............................... 13

3 Completely His 25

4 Your Body: Temple of the Holy Spirit...................... 37

5 Your Body: Earthly Instrument for Service 49

6 Nourish the Body... 61

7 Move the Body 73

8 Rest, Renew, Revitalize:
   The Sabbath Rhythm 85

9 A Healthy Mind 97

10 Handling Stress: The Silent Killer 109

11 Eliminating Toxic Emotions.................................121

12 *Well2Serve* 133

Bibliography and Abbrevations for Well*Facts* 149

Appendix A 155

Acknowledgements

I want to thank Jim Anthony for inviting me to write a Biblical foundation for his new initiative to help others achieve total wellness for the purpose of service. I have known Jim for nearly a decade and during that time I have grown to embrace his passion for wellness and service. This small book is part of a much larger initiative called *Well2Win*. Please take a moment and visit the website www.well2win.com to help you understand the balanced Biblical approach that drives *Well2Win*.

There are books on the market that deal with diet, exercise, rest, and other assorted health topics, but I have not seen anything that brings all these elements together in one place. Further, this is a unique emphasis because Jim believes that success in life is found in serving our Creator by serving others. For that reason, every element of total wellness is addressed with the end result being our effective service to others.

I have enjoyed working with other members of the *Well2Win* team and they have added immeasurably to the content of this small Bible study which serves as an introduction and a stimulus to join us on a wellness journey that will change your life and the lives of others you impact.

This book is published by Auxano Press and serves as part of our non-disposable curriculum for study in small groups. We believe that nothing changes one's thinking and thus one's life but the Word of God applied by the Spirit of God. Therefore, this material is unapologetically Biblical in its orientation. Once you study this book, we encourage you to keep it in your library or pass it on to a friend. It is best to study it with a small group of friends who will keep you accountable for learning and applying the truths of Scripture. Study guides and administrative helps are available free from Auxanopress.com.

My wife and partner in ministry, Paula, is my greatest encourager. My children and grandchildren continue to motivate me to put Biblical truths into print. For the sake of readability, footnotes in the Biblical exposition are kept to a minimum. The quotations in the section called Well*facts* are found in the bibliography and on our web site *Well2Win*.

INTRODUCTION

All of us have set goals without seeing the results we desire. The reason most of us fall short—very simply—we do not have the support, encouragement, incentives, accountability, and information we need to be truly successful.

Knowing exactly what we need to be successful on the journey to wellness, *Well2Win* aligns doctors, insurance, employees, friends, and family to create a culture that fosters positive life-style changes that will put you on the path to a life of vitality and service. This alignment creates a force so strong—we guarantee your success if you bring only one thing—a burning desire and commitment to live well and serve others.

The lives most Americans lead are paradoxically fast-paced and yet sedentary. We work hard, eat fast food, endure high stress, and spend hours each week unwinding in front of the television with bowls full of sugary or salty snacks. We go to bed late and wake up early so we can repeat the process.

If you want to make a positive and lasting change to improve your health and the quality of your life, you are going to be swimming against the tide of our culture. Many of us have assumed we are doomed to a life of mediocrity because we lack the motivation, information, and support to make the life-style changes necessary to be *Well2Win*.

Well2Win is about leveling the playing field. This little book can have a big impact! But it is only the beginning. We have highly trained coaches who will come along side you and your friends and family to train you to develop and refine the skills you need to be victorious. Welcome to your new life!

Jim Anthony
Amanda Stilwell

Uniquely Created for Kingdom Service

CHAPTER 1

Focal Text: Genesis 1:26–31

Judging by the weight loss ads and health care news we see on television, you'd think our main reason for wanting to stay active and fit is merely to improve our appearance, or to fend off the effects of aging and Alzheimer's, or to lower our insurance premiums and our burden on the public good. But long before the invention of dietary supplements and elliptical machines, God had already established the primary motivation behind all our efforts at healthy living.

"In the beginning," the Bible says, He created us for His work.

"Let Us make man in Our image," He said, "according to Our likeness; and let them rule over the fish of the sea and over the birds of the sky and over the cattle and over all the earth, and over every creeping thing that creeps on the earth" (Gen. 1:26). We are of inestimable worth and meaning to God, in both our design and our duties.

We are made in His image.

Fashioned after His likeness.

Endowed with responsibilities for managing all of creation.

And because He has invested so much of Himself in us, and has personally entrusted us with such important work to accomplish, we now possess the greatest motivation of all for keeping ourselves strong in body, soul, and spirit: to maximize the years and energy we bring to this vital task, and to worship the One who has chosen, beyond all logic, to value us so highly.

That's the foundation behind this entire study.

In the Beginning

When you read the first words of the Bible—"In the beginning"—what goes through your mind? Do you think of it as little more than the introductory phrase from a good fairy tale—"Once upon a time?" I'm afraid we can read it so quickly and casually that we overlook its fundamental significance.

It is true that the phrase "in the beginning" declares the inauguration of all things, but it is much more than a simple marking of time. The same Hebrew word from which we derive "beginning" can also be translated as "choice" or "first fruits." Therefore, we can appropriately refer to creation as God's gift to Himself—the "first fruits" of His divine activity on earth. And we can rightly consider ourselves, by virtue of His own will and purpose, the main feature of His entire performance.

But even this enhanced interpretation can only scratch the surface of the deep, life-changing truths embedded within the narrative of creation. For example:

"In the beginning" means there is more to come. God created all things with intentionality and purpose—the heavens, the earth, the sky, the seas, the plants, the starry hosts, the animals, and ultimately man—creating it by Himself, for Himself. And implicit within this truth is the idea that God continues to be personally involved in His handiwork, driving and directing what the "more" will be. He remains just as active in our lives today as at the beginning of recorded time. This is why we, too, should think of ourselves as fully engaged with Him, personally involved in His purposeful activity. Life is a journey to be traveled, both with Him and with others.

"In the beginning" anticipates life's ultimate end. God created the heavens and the earth with the future in mind—the reconciliation of "all things to Himself" through Christ (Col. 1:20). Life is going somewhere, toward a meaningful conclusion, a culmination point when God's kingdom will be fully established. And you were created with the potential to join Him in this reality.

"In the beginning" means the Creator is the Owner. Not only is creation a divine activity; it is a statement of divine ownership. The subject of creation is always God, and everything else is a direct object. All of nature, all material things, all the way down to our own bodies—all of it belongs to Him. So whatever the nature of your birth, you are not here by mistake. You are here because your Creator desired you to be here. And this fact gives Him rightful authority over your life.

What would change for you if you truly lived according to these truths, knowing that He designed everything He made—yourself included—to serve His kingdom purpose?

It Was Very Good

As the story of creation unfolds, we find God systematically preparing the world for life's myriad possibilities and for man's habitation. At each point, He stands back and affirms that what He made is "good." The first chapter of Genesis alone contains seven

3

distinct pronouncements of the goodness of the created world (vv. 4, 10, 12, 18, 21, 25, 31). God declared the light "good" because it dispelled the darkness that had once characterized the earth. He declared the vegetation "good" as it burst into bloom and covered the earth with beauty. All created things are from God, and therefore they are good because they reflect His character, because they declare His glory, and because He has assigned value and meaning to everything He has made.

The entirety of the Bible affirms the goodness of God's world. Its bounty is designed not only to meet our needs but also to bring joy to our hearts. The psalmist declared, "He causes the grass to grow for the cattle, and vegetation for the labor of man, so that he may bring forth food from the earth, and wine which makes man's heart glad, so that he may make his face glisten with oil, and food which sustains man's heart" (Ps. 104:14–15). Solomon joins the refrain, "I know that there is nothing better for them than to rejoice and enjoy the good life. It also is the gift of God whenever anyone eats, drinks, and enjoys all his efforts" (Eccles. 3:12–13 hcsb).

It's all good.

But following the final act of creation—when God created man in His own image—His assessment of the entirety of His work doubled in value. Each individual part of creation was "good," He had said. But the whole of it? With man as its centerpiece?

It was "very good" (Gen. 1:31).

This superlative statement leads us to the profound truth that inspires this study. If mankind has been created, male and female, in the image of God, and has been esteemed with such an enormous amount of worth by the Creator Himself, the ramifications of how we treat and consider the health and well-being of our human dwellings—our bodies—are dramatic.

Man in the Image of God

It is impossible to read the first chapter of Genesis and not realize that man is the zenith of creation. Nothing else on earth can claim the birthright of being made in the image of God. Man was singled out by God to enjoy a special, personal relationship with Him and the created world. We are His agents on earth. We are the world's caretakers.

When you read Genesis 1:24–31, you notice that man shares the sixth day of creation with other living creatures, such as livestock, crawling things, and wildlife. All of these are made from the same "stuff" as man—the dust of the earth (2:7, 19)—and are given a similar command from their Creator: to reproduce after their kind (1:22–28). But the main emphasis is not on the similarities but on the unique differences. Genesis 1:24, in referring to the creation of animal life, uses the phrase, "Let the earth bring forth living creatures." But in regard to man, this phrase is replaced in verse 26 with "Let us make"—in the very image of God.

Biblical scholars differ somewhat on the significance of the plural pronoun "Our" in verse 26—"Let us make man in Our image, according to Our likeness." Some see the plural as a way of underlining the sovereign majesty of God. Others see an implicit affirmation of the triune nature of God, who expresses the unity of

His one nature in three persons—Father, Son, and Holy Spirit. In either case, we can all agree that God created the world for man's habitation and then created mankind in His own image.

But what does being made in His image mean? Here are at least three conclusions:

1. Man is a relational being. In Genesis 2, which is a recounting of the creation story with the spotlight on man, God declares, "It is not good for the man to be alone" (v. 18). The next two verses show the first man, Adam, naming the animals, after which we read the curious statement, "There was not found a helper suitable for him" (v. 20). On the surface, this picture is a bit humorous—the idea that an appropriate partner for man could possibly be found among the animals parading past him. But the point is clear: only someone created like himself, created in the image of God, can be "bone of my bones and flesh of my flesh" (v. 23a). We have been designed and destined to seek relationship with others created in the image of God.

Throughout this study you will be challenged to build your wellness team from family members, church members, and friends.

But our greatest relational need is to live in intimate and personal relationship with our Creator, as seen in Genesis 3:8, where Adam and Eve hear "the sound of the Lord God walking in the garden in the cool of the day." This tells us that God created them (and us) with the capacity and desire to know and serve Him. In fact, we cannot live fully without Him because we have been created by Him and for Him.

2. Man is a rational being. Simply stated, we have

been created with the capacity to understand and respond to God's revelation. The garden that Adam and Eve inhabited was designed to foster the full development of their spiritual, physical, and aesthetic appetites. Prior to the fall, they enjoyed full and unhindered fellowship with God, free to eat from every tree but one—the tree of the knowledge of good and evil (2:16–17). We have no indication that the animals were given a restriction of any kind—no divine word containing both command and prohibition. Why? Because they lacked the capacity to comprehend and understand their Creator in the same way as man does. Man is unique in that he can both hear God and willfully respond to Him.

This rational ability is the basis for the revelation of God to man—the Bible. The Bible is unique in that its content originates with God (revelation) and was communicated by God to man (inspiration). It is both a truthful (inerrant) and a reliable (infallible) guide for the living of one's life. It not only contains the historical story of God's redemptive work among man, but also contains our guideline for successful living.

3. Man is a responsible being. God's first spoken words to the man and woman were words of blessing followed by an assignment. "God blessed them; and God said to them, 'Be fruitful and multiply, and fill the earth, and subdue it; and rule over the fish of the sea and over the birds of the sky and over every living thing that moves on the earth'" (1:28).

The idea of responsibility is implied in both the blessing and the assignment, as is its partner: accountability. Man was given dominion over the created order, implying that he was responsible for managing it according to the design and desire of its Creator, caring for it as God's royal representatives, ruling the earth in His place. The words "subdue" and "rule" in verse 28 do not imply possession. We find no suggestion anywhere in Scripture that God transferred ownership of the earth to man. Ours is a delegated ownership. We have secondary dominion under the absolute dominion of our Lord, the Creator and Owner.

So within the creation context, we see all three elements of man's uniqueness—relational, rational, responsible—coming together to comprise man's role as steward. As relational beings, we desire and need fellowship with God and with others created in His image. As rational beings, we understand His revelation, which provides us His standards for the proper use of all His resources. Thus we have been made responsible for managing the King's resources in accordance with His desires.

And part of this command, as well as its privilege, is the care and keeping of ourselves—body, mind, and spirit.

The process we are calling *Well2Serve* is based on these scriptural principles, and thus is not simply another wellness program designed to help you look better in a bathing suit. It is instead a plan for living by God's pattern to achieve maximum potential in His service. By utilizing this truth as the driving force behind your complete desire for wellness, you will discover new freedom and inspiration in all your efforts.

You are unique and special. No one on this planet has your precise DNA, your fingerprints, or your precise set of gifts and talents. God created you for Himself and for the advancement of His purposes on earth. The task and goal of this study is to show you Biblical principles for the personal management of your entire life so that you can be the very best of what God intended you to be, enabling you to serve Him with joy and effectiveness.

Memorize the following verse and meditate daily on its astounding truth.

For Memory and Meditation

I will give thanks to You, for I am fearfully and wonderfully made" (Ps. 139:14a).

WELL*FACTS*

We are created with a desire to do things—just like God. The brain allows us to process things and to create things. When we learn, when we work, when we strategize, when we do things, it is God in us urging us to create and imitate His own handiwork that He created at the beginning of time. Hayles, 128.

The spiritual dimension has to do with my seeking God, my understanding God, my getting close to God, my understanding my purpose, why I am here to serve, and to seek Him. Hayles, 124.

Another way to think about your genetic inheritance: its stored information, the factory-installed information that comes with your biological system. You have the power—with your behavior software—to alter that information along the way. But if you don't take any action, then the stored information is what dictates how the genes play out. Roizen, 21.

I believe it is especially important for people to own up to feelings of guilt and shame in their own hearts. This is a vital key to unlocking health and wholeness. Colbert, 90.

I realize that group is the medicine, the community is the cure. Hyman, 165.

That is the power of social group, the power of the group as medicine. The right information delivered in a fun curriculum through a social group has the power to turn our obesity and diabetes epidemic around. Hyman, 167.

WELL*ACTS*

You were created by God to live in perfect fellowship with Him. If you are not sure about how you can have a relationship with God, go to Appendix A.

You will be introduced throughout this study to information concerning your wellness as a physical person created in God's image. As a rational being, you will be able to understand the principles being shared with you. As a responsible being, you will be held accountable for this information. Stop right now and ask the Father to open your ears and your heart to hear and obey the truths you will learn from His Word.

As a relational being, you are created for community. Evidence indicates that learning and responding in community promotes success. If you are reading this material alone, find a companion and hold each other accountable. If you are studying this as part of a small group, make a commitment to be faithful and accountable.

Throughout the study, you will be reminded that you are a physical being who functions in the realm of the emotional, the spiritual, and the intellectual. You are an integrated whole, and it is therefore important that you take each section with equal seriousness and ask the Lord to show you areas where you need transformation.

Sign this covenant. "With God's help and the support of my team, I will complete this study and make the life-style changes necessary to be *Well2Serve*.

The Two Great Commandments

CHAPTER 2

Focal Text: Mark 12:28–34

If you were asked to give a succinct summary of what it means to follow God and be faithful to Him, what would you say? Could you boil it all down into a single, core statement? That's precisely what an expert in the law asked of Jesus one day.

Actually this entire passage from Mark 12—all the way back to verse 13—shows people asking Him knotty, complex questions, seeking to trap Him in His own words, hoping to create enough controversy to curb the crowd's thirst for this itinerant teacher. First the Pharisees (legalists) and Herodians (supporters of Rome) asked Him a hot-button question about the paying of taxes to Caesar. Then a number of Sadducees asked Him what the nature of people's marital status would be like in the hereafter—a strange question, seeing that the Sadducees didn't believe in a bodily resurrection from the dead anyway.

So the question which follows from the scribe (an expert in Old Testament law) in verse 28 should be seen as no less crafty and hypocritical: "What commandment is the foremost of all?" He knew there were many commandments to choose from. And no matter which way Jesus answered, there was no end of opportunity for finding fault with Him.

Yet Jesus' response was so simple and profound, it put a stop to all other questions for the rest of the day. And it remains to this day a big part of why we understand that His calling on our lives goes far beyond a mere spiritual sense.

He began with the first words of the Shema, the ancient Jewish confession of faith, a trusted declaration of God's oneness and sovereignty found in Old Testament Scripture—"The Lord is our God, the Lord is One," followed by man's fitting response, "You shall love the Lord your God with all your heart and with all your soul and with all your might" (Deut. 6:4–5). No one in any of the groups who were gathered around Jesus that day, including those curious members of the crowd, would have dared dispute this doctrinal affirmation. But then Jesus carried it further, adding a second commandment of equal importance: "You shall love your neighbor as yourself" (Mark 12:31)—a partial quotation from Leviticus 19:18, and a natural corollary to one's authentic love for God.

Not only was the scribe unable to argue against Jesus' logic, he actually found himself agreeing with it, adding that these two commandments were more important than even the making of burnt offerings and sacrifices (v. 33). Matthew's account of this event additionally reveals Jesus declaring that "on these two commandments depend the whole Law and the Prophets" (Matt. 22:40). In other words, they summarize the entire Old Testament teaching on what it means to fully love God.

And so, in the space of a few memorable words, Jesus confirmed that His calling on our lives is more than just spiritual. When He speaks of loving God, He is speaking of our entire being. Nothing excluded. He both demands and deserves every inch of us. Which in some cases may even mean having a few inches less of us!

The Christian life is a comprehensive life.

God Wants All of You

Some people seem to think that Christian commitment can be added on to an already overcrowded life in the same way we might add another line to our résumé. We can become quite adept at compartmentalizing our lives as if Christianity only affects what we do or say on Sunday.

Nothing, however, could be further from the truth.

God's covenant love for us involves our whole person. After all, He doesn't just redeem us in individual portions—our hearts but not our bodies, our souls but not our minds; therefore, we should not offer back to Him only select parts of ourselves. We should seek Him and love Him with a passionate single-mindedness, placing our entire selves at His disposal—our thoughts, actions, and activities, as well as our exercise and our rest.

When we give Him only bits and pieces of ourselves, we suffer from religious schizophrenia—a tragic spiritual disease that not only brings us up short of our calling but also leads to discouragement, inner turmoil, and a lack of effective service. We cannot interact with Him at one moment of the day or week, yet not make regular connections from what we've read and heard in Scripture to our work, our play, our bodies, and our interpersonal relationships.

Here's how Paul states this principle of loving God with one's total being: "Therefore I urge you, brethren, by the mercies of God, to present your bodies a living and holy sacrifice, acceptable to God, which is your spiritual service of worship. And do not be conformed to this world, but be transformed by the renewing of your mind, so that you may prove what the will of God is, that which is good and acceptable and perfect" (Rom. 12:1–2).

Notice the progression. He actually tells us to start with our bodies first, which establishes the platform for God to transform our mind, which then impacts our ability to know and accomplish His will. That's why even the presentation of our bodies to Him can legitimately be called our "spiritual service of worship."

The word "spiritual" can also mean "logical." The submitting of our bodies to Him each day, making them available to Him for His purposes, should be seen as a sensical response to God's act of redeeming us. Since we have received the "mercies of God," we should therefore consider the health and purity of our physical bodies as an important part of our thankful praise.

In other words, this is normal Christianity.

And what's more, as your surrendered body leads you to think with a transformed mind, this gift of yourself to God has already been declared by Him to be "good and acceptable and perfect." Many Christians seem to be paralyzed by feelings of inadequacy in serving God. But trust His Word: you are all that He wants! God rewards your availability with the gift of supernatural ability.

Love God with All Your Heart

Since the depths of our love for God should truly involve our entire person—heart, soul, mind, and

16

strength—let's consider these various aspects of our identity one at a time, seeing how we can serve Him faithfully in each respect.

When the Bible speaks of the heart, it refers to the core of one's being, the command center of life, the place that controls feelings, emotions, desires, and passions. This is where religious commitment is established, and therefore the new creation is said to begin in our heart.

Ezekiel, an Old Testament prophet, speaks of how God can remove from us a "heart of stone" and replace it with a "heart of flesh," responsive to the word of God (11:19–20). This new heart that longs for God is not like the old one that led us into sin and away from Him (v. 21). When we are saved, we receive a new heart, which means we are new persons. The Holy Spirit now indwells us, enabling us to love God completely.

We cannot underestimate the importance of this transformation, nor fail to realize what our hearts are capable of doing when our love turns inward. In His condemnation of the Pharisees, Jesus quotes Isaiah, "This people honors me with their lips, but their heart is far away from me" (Mark 7:6). Later in that same chapter, Jesus further clarifies the nature of our hearts: "For from within, out of the heart of men, proceed the evil thoughts, fornications, thefts, murders, and adulteries, deeds of coveting and wickedness, as well as deceit, sensuality, envy, slander, pride and foolishness. All these evil things proceed from within and defile the man" (vv. 21–23).

So we must be very careful, knowing the potential of what all can be generated from our hearts, that we cultivate its God-given ability for loving Him. Jesus taught His followers that whatever a person treasures most will determine the passion of his or her heart (Matt. 6:21). Therefore, He alone must be our chief treasure. To love Him with all our heart means that we place Him at the center of every aspect of our lives. We ascribe to Him rightful authority over our feelings, emotions, desires, and passions. And we do it every day. If we expect to love Him with all our hearts, He must be the core focus of our lives.

Love God with All Your Soul

In the creation narrative, we are told that God breathed into man the breath of life, and man became a living "soul" or "being" (Gen. 2:7). The soul refers to the animating force of life, the vital essence of man. And while this concept can be somewhat difficult to grasp and define, our purpose in studying it is not to overly isolate it. We as humans are not divided up so neatly and distinctly into component parts; our nature is a united whole. The soul is definitely important, and its place is integral in both our existence and our worship, but we can expect to see some overlap in the roles of mind, soul, and spirit.

"Soul" refers to the entire human being in terms of physical life which requires daily sustenance. Jesus told the disciples, for example, they did not need to worry about their "soul" concerning what they eat or drink. The cure for such earthly anxiety? He gave them two answers: an awareness that their Father knew their needs and was able to meet them (Matt. 6:32), and a commitment to seek His kingdom and righteousness as first priority (v. 33). This passage does not suggest that we should be unconcerned about our physical body, the longings of our soul. It simply means that our need for food, clothing, money, time, and all the other necessities of life are God's business to provide. And as He does—working through our cooperation—we should view them as resources not to consume but to be invested in work of His kingdom.

The word "soul" can also be used to speak of one's feelings, wishes, and will. The soul can desire evil (Prov. 21:10), for example, but it can also seek after God (Ps. 42:2–3). The soul has such a wide range of emotions, in fact, that it can be spoken of as being incited, embittered, unsettled, or kept in suspense. The Bible speaks of the bitter soul of the childless, the sick, or the threatened. The soul can also express positive emotions too. It rejoices, praises, hopes, and exhibits patience.

Thus, loving God with our soul means we surrender to Him our emotions, just as we surrender our worry over basic needs. We replace anxiety, bitterness, and willful disobedience with joy, praise, and hopeful surrender.

Love God with All Your Mind

The mind allows us to think, perceive, and reflect. It directs our judgments and opinions. But can it love? Can we love God with our intellect? Absolutely! In fact, a wholehearted love for God demands it. Tragically, many believers attempt to feed their entire Christian experience with an emotion-laden diet that pays little attention to the development of their reason and mental acumen.

Peter instructs believers to "sanctify Christ as Lord in your hearts, always being ready to make a defense to everyone who asks you to give an account for the hope that is in you, yet with gentleness and reverence" (1 Pet. 3:15). Did you notice the linking of the heart and mind in this passage? To sanctify Christ as Lord in our hearts requires that we prepare our minds to explain who He is and what He's done for us.

Paul exhorted young Timothy, "Be diligent to present yourself approved to God as a workman who does not need to be ashamed, accurately handling the word of truth" (2 Tim. 2:15). Loving God with all our mind requires that we read and study God's Word along with other good books. Numerous studies have documented the importance of keeping one's mind active and growing. And if we're interested in exercising our mind for the purpose of improving our memory or becoming articulate on current events, why not for greater praise, service, and love of God?

Love God with All Your Strength

Mark includes in Jesus' call to love God with all our heart, soul, and mind, the added phrase "with all your strength." Strength refers to our physical capacities. We have already looked at Romans 12:1, which commands us to present our "bodies" as a living sacrifice. When we do so, we are placing at His disposal all of our gifts and abilities, since—think of it—the human body provides the only platform from which the spiritual gifts function. Therefore, our bodies are the only instrument for serving God and others. No wonder God wants our bodies at full strength!

Paul uses numerous athletic images to talk about the intensity of his service to the Lord. In 1 Corinthians 9:24–27, he speaks of running to win the race, exercising self-control and discipline over his body so that his work will not be disqualified. We will discuss this matter in greater detail in chapter 4, but suffice to say that we cannot ignore our diet and exercise as if they are irrelevant in our loving service to God.

What if you could add both years and vitality to your life through the proper physical care of your body? Would that not make you a more effective servant of the Lord? Of course it would! So to claim to be wholehearted in our love for God, yet ignore the importance of this physical body, is an absurdity. Your body is God's gift to you as you join Him in expanding His kingdom to the world.

Are you beginning to sense the radical nature of this study and its potential impact? It will change your life and allow you to change the world!

For Memory and Meditation

"You shall love the Lord your God with all your heart, and with all your soul, and with all your mind, and with all your strength" (Mark 12:30).

WELL*FACTS*

"Mind, body, and spirit act in concert to determine health and wellbeing." Carl Thorsen in Urban, ch.17

We are physical begins fashioned by our Creator to do things according to His will and purpose. We are physical entities that operate in many dimensions. We operate in the spiritual, the emotional, and the intellectual. All these dimensions are expected to operate in kind or in sync with each other. All of these dimensions are expected to be catalysts to help us attain a holistic and wholesome life. Hayles, 53.

Mother Teresa said that the greatest disease of mankind is the absence of love. The kind of love that truly heals us emotionally and physically is not romantic love, but rather the unconditional love that comes from God. The love that heals is not sexual in nature, but spiritual. Colbert, 213.

In recent years neuroscientists have discovered that the heart has its own independent nervous system. At least forty thousand nerve cells (neurons) exist in the human heart. These abundant nerve cells give it thinking, feeling capacity.... The heart's "brain" and the nervous system relay messages back and forth to the brain in the skull, creating a two-way communication between these two organs. The ultimate "real you" is a composite of what your heart tells your brain, your brain tells your heart, and your will decides to believe say and do. Colbert, 141–142.

WELL*ACTS*

Can you say that you love God with all your heart? What area of your feelings, desires, or passions are you withholding from Him?

Do you love God with your entire mind? Complete the reading of this book, and start a habit of reading inspirational and uplifting materials.

The mind needs to be exercised. One way is by improving your memory. Memorize the twelve verses listed at the end of each chapter. We will use them later for meditation. As your memory improves, memorize entire chapters of the Bible.

Since the thoughts and emotions are critical components of our total wellness, confess to God thoughts and emotions which are not consistent with the truths of Scripture. Ask Him to give you the strength to think of those things which are pure and holy.

Keep a journal in which you record ways in which your thought processes are self-destructive. Confess each as sin and ask God to replace them with His thoughts about you.

Refuse to use words like "stupid," "idiot," or "loser," even in your mind, to describe yourself. Replace destructive words with life-giving ones.

Completely His

CHAPTER 3

Focal Text: 1 Thessalonians 5:23–24

"Sanctification" is a term that may sound a bit dated to our contemporary ears, but it is an important and beautiful concept that speaks not only of our redemption but also of our worth as an instrument through whom God works. You were created with purpose, redeemed at a great price, and chosen and empowered to join God as He completes His earthly kingdom activity.

Does it excite you to think that you are an instrument God desires to use? Does it intimidate you a little? Do you wonder if you are worthy or capable of accomplishing anything of such eternal value?

In any case, I believe you'll enjoy today's study. Paul was writing to the church at Thessalonica, a church he had planted while on his second missionary journey (Acts 17). As was often the case, he had been forced to leave Thessalonica quickly because of mounting hostility and growing opposition. So he wrote this letter to give them further instruction, correcting some of their misunderstandings and inspiring the believers to stand firm in their faith.

But in his concluding benediction, he left behind a message that continues to encourage believers of every generation as they contemplate their earthly service for the King of kings. For if God has chosen to cover us so completely in His sanctifying power (heart, soul, mind, and body) and has promised that He Himself will be faithful to accomplish His work within us,

25

we are left with little to fear—and with nothing that cannot be offered up to Him for His purposes.

The God of Peace Himself

Paul begins this final paragraph by praying that the "God of peace Himself" will "sanctify" his readers, and that He will do it "entirely." Before we tackle the larger concept of sanctification, let's look at the significance of just this first phrase—"the God of peace Himself."

The use of "Himself" immediately following the reference to "the God of peace" indicates God's personal involvement in the process of our sanctification. Be careful not to minimize what this entails. God, who obviously is able to do anything He pleases, delights in focusing His attention on us—not to condemn us, but to complete us, to help us, to enable us. The inclusion of the word "Himself" also indicates that God alone can accomplish this process of sanctification in our lives and that He guarantees its full completion.

"God of peace," by the way, is a term Paul frequently uses at the end of his letters (cf. 2 Thess. 3:16; Rom. 15:33; 16:20; 2 Cor. 13:11; Phil. 4:9), just as he mentions the word "peace" in his opening greeting here: "Grace to you and peace" (1:1). Sometimes we use the word "peace" to simply mean the cessation of war or conflict. But the Hebrew word *shalom* is much broader. It signifies "wholeness," and thus speaks of prosperity in its broadest sense, the total flourishing of the soul. And because the bestowal of this gift on His people is so characteristic of God, Paul can rightly call Him the "God of peace."

Sanctify You Entirely

Now that we've looked at who does the sanctifying in our lives, let's see what sanctification is all about. Paul often speaks of Christians as "saints." This word comes from the same root as the word translated "sanctify." The essential idea of sanctification is that of being set apart for God's service. In the Old Testament, the golden vessels that were placed in the tabernacle were "sanctified" or "set apart" for God's service. They weren't just ordinary; they were special. They had a particular use.

But while "set apart for service" is the primary idea of sanctification, it can also refer to the character or purity of the vessel which is dedicated. Since God is holy, the vessels which serve Him are to reflect His pristine character.

The theme of sanctification is a major emphasis of this first letter to the Thessalonians. In 2:12, for instance, the idea of sanctification is clearly present, even though the word itself is not used: "so that you would walk in a manner worthy of the God who calls you into His own kingdom and glory." This is why you and I have been set apart—for His kingdom (His rule) and His glory.

Glory is a word often sung, said, and preached in spiritual settings, but not always so clearly understood. "Glory" speaks of God's manifest presence. In the Old Testament, God's glory was seen in phenomena such as the burning bush or the flaming, smoking mountain of Sinai—external indicators of His identity and activity. But with the coming of Jesus, the glory of God moved indoors. John declares: "And the Word became flesh, and dwelt among us, and we saw His glory, glory as of the only begotten from the Father, full of grace and truth" (John 1:14). Jesus possessed glory within Himself. And as those who have received His indwelling Spirit, we too can display His glorious presence through our daily lives. To bring Him glory by living under His kingdom rule is one objective of our sanctification.

A second purpose is to love. Paul prays at one point that he may return to Thessalonica so that he can "complete what is lacking in your faith" (1 Thess. 3:10). Part of this completion includes an increase in their love for "one another" and for "all people." (vv. 11–13).

Another purpose is our purity—which Paul makes clear by repeating the term "sanctification" three times in the space of four verses. In 4:3 he declares, "For this is the will of God, your sanctification; that is, that you abstain from sexual immorality." Once again, in verse 4, he mentions sexual purity as a distinguishing mark between believers and unbelievers. He broadens the concept in verse 7: "For God has not called us for the purpose of impurity, but in sanctification." He then concludes this section of teaching in verse 8 with the solemn warning that anyone who rejects his instruction is not rejecting man but God, who has provided us His Spirit to enable the sanctifying work in us.

Then we come to our primary text in 5:23, where we are told that God will sanctify us "entirely." The word translated "entirely" or "wholly" in some English translations is a unique compound word which is found only here in the New Testament. The idea is that of "wholeness" and "completion." God sanctifies you so you can be whole—a complete person! Sanctification is an ongoing process which God promises to both start and finish, rendering us blameless "at the coming of our Lord Jesus Christ" (5:23). When you get discouraged while in the process of sanctification, take heart—because God has promised He will complete this task in you.

By gathering all of these themes together, we can identify several key takeaways concerning sanctification. First, it is God's will for all believers. Second, it involves our whole being, including our thoughts and actions. Third, in the deepest sense it can only be accomplished by God. Both here and in Romans 15:16, the work of sanctification is attributed to the Holy Spirit. In Ephesians 5:26, it is ascribed to Christ. In other words, sanctification is so important that the entire Godhead is involved in the process.

But still, despite His exclusive ability to accomplish it, God has chosen to incorporate a human element into our sanctification. We must yield ourselves to it. Sanctification is not an option; it is our calling. It is not a burden to be borne; it is a privilege to be pursued—with all that is within us—all for His glory.

All of You—Spirit, Soul, and Body

"May your spirit and soul and body be preserved complete" (v. 24). Many people see in this phrase an obvious description of the trichotomy of the human personality—spirit, soul, and body. Others argue for a dichotomy, asserting that soul and spirit are basically one and the same. But by anyone's interpretation, Paul is undoubtedly arguing that man in his entirety must be presented to God as a pure vessel for service. So whenever we limit ourselves to thinking about sanctification in terms of our spiritual lives alone, ignoring the other dimensions of God's desire to "sanctify us entirely," we miss out on the all day, everyday experience of being set apart for Him head to toe, in and out — each part of us dedicated for His glory.

Perhaps most surprising for many of Paul's readers would have been his emphasis on the body. Greeks considered the body a tomb or prison of the immortal soul. Therefore, the ultimate fate of the body was of little importance to many in the first century. For Paul, however, there was no existence or service apart from the body. In Romans 12:1-2 (as we've seen), Paul insists that the presentation of our body as a living sacrifice is that which God desires and has already declared to be our reasonable and acceptable offering to Him. But don't stop there: look at the following verses (3–8), where Paul discusses the spiritual gifts which are distributed to each one of us for the purpose of serving God through His body, the church. Like we said, if not for healthy, nourished, able bodies, we have very few ways of putting these spiritual gifts into practice.

So the body is equally as important in our service to Him as every other part. Note the significance, in fact, that even after death we will continue to dwell within a body—a resurrected body which is imperishable, glorious, and spiritual in nature (1 Cor. 15). This implies continuity between our current body and our heavenly body.

Spirit, soul, and body—complete.
On earth as it is in heaven—complete.

And by the time we arrive there, we will realize to our delighted wonder that we have been sanctified to such a complete extent that we are truly "without blame" before Him by His grace.

God's goal, therefore, is not for us to live a good life; He desires for us to live an exceptional life—not one of sinless perfection, but of discovering and fulfilling the purpose for which God has created us. We are to serve Him faithfully until He comes, assured that He will continue His work in us until the return of Christ . . . when all will be made complete.

Until the Coming of the Lord

Reading this letter in its entirety, you find that the second coming of the Lord was an issue of great interest to its recipients. Some were in need of comfort because of the recent loss of a loved one (4:13–18), while others were mostly interested in speculations concerning "the times and the epochs" of Christ's return (5:1–11), apparently with little regard for how its impact applied to everyday life. To those who were grieving, Paul assures them that the promised return of the Lord means their grief can be lightened by the presence of genuine hope (4:13). And for those caught up in speculation, he declares they already know enough—even without knowing everything—to continue encouraging one another and building each other up. Since a faithful God is sure to fulfill His word, their job was simply to stay busy serving Him without worrying about the mysterious details of the future.

Why, though, would Paul choose to discuss sanctification in the context of the coming of Christ? First, sanctification does not occur suddenly and magically at the coming of the Lord unless we are already "saints" by virtue of redemption, unless we are seeking holiness through our yieldedness to His Spirit. This part of our sanctification (our current separation for service) is in progress now and will remain in progress until the coming of the Lord.

But there is more! For when our earthly service is complete, our eternal service begins without any interruption. God is at work in us until His coming in the person of His Son, and He will continue to work in us for all eternity.

All too often I encounter some of our senior saints who live with the impression that when they retired from work, they also retired from service to the King through His bride, the church. The idea seems to be that they've done their time, that it's up to the next generation to take over now. But retirement from secular employment simply provides more time for service. For this reason, it is critical that we keep our bodies—the human platform for the use of our gifts— in top physical and emotional condition. We must be *Well2Serve*.

Faithful Is He Who Calls You

Finally, just in case you feel a little overwhelmed, questioning your ability to be entirely set apart for God's use, this final reminder is for you. "Faithful is He who calls you, and He also will bring it to pass" (5:24). Our effective service is only possible through God's power, and it is assured because He will make certain it happens.

What God calls us to do, He will do through us. The Caller is the Doer. You can do it, because He will do it through you! You can make a difference! Your life matters!

So my advice to you—in the words of Paul—is to "rejoice always; pray without ceasing; in everything give thanks; for this is God's will for you in Christ Jesus. Do not quench the Spirit; do not despise prophetic utterances. But examine everything carefully; hold fast to that which is good; abstain from every form of evil" (1 Thess. 5:16–22).

Be completely His.

For Memory and Meditation

"Now may the God of peace Himself sanctify you entirely; and may your spirit and soul and body be preserved complete, without blame at the coming of our Lord Jesus Christ" (1 Thess. 5:23).

WELL*FACTS*

The Scriptures teach us how to live and love fully. But somehow we skip over the parts that instruct us to honor the vessel of the Holy Spirit, our body. Warren, 77

This means that my spiritual, intellectual, and emotional dimensions need to be regenerated for His purpose, for His use, and to His liking. Hayles, 129.

Your body is the living reality of everything you are, and everything you experience happens to all of you, not just to your brain. Colbert, 44.

"If you choose not to forgive someone, I guarantee that your toxic deadly emotions of resentment and hatred will continue to poison your system in ways that are just as dangerous as your taking in a literal poison. Not only will your body suffer, but your mind, spirit, and your general emotional well-being will suffer." Colbert, 170.

The psychological is as important a part of who you are as your physical existence. One does not survive without the other. The emotional is driven by the psychological, but not to the detriment of the spiritual. The spiritual requires a surrender of all things, whether physical, intellectual, or psychological to God so that He can make us into who we truly are and what we should truly be. Hayles, 100.

Sanctification means the believer becoming more like Christ. Sanctification begins with our surrender to God. Is there an area of life which you have failed to present to God? Simply bow your head and offer it to Him.

Sanctification is a process and not a simple one-time commitment. God has promised that He is faithful to bring it to pass.

1 Thessalonians 5:23 provides several helpful steps that will help us stay faithful to the process—seek good for one another, rejoice always, pray without ceasing, and give thanks in everything. Adopt these simple steps today:

Find an accountability partner for the duration of this study. Form a team and celebrate your acheivements to date.

Focus each day on the small blessings for which you can rejoice.

Remain in a posture and attitude of prayer. You should begin with praise and thanksgiving, focus on how you can advance His kingdom, and bring your smallest requests to Him.

Set aside regular moments to offer thanks, not only to God but to others who bring blessing into your life. The attitude of gratitude has a healing quality. Regularly journal your progress in all areas of the *Well2Serve* process.

Believe in your uniqueness!

Your Body: Temple of the Holy Spirit

CHAPTER 4

Focal Text: 1 Corinthians 6:12–20

As the old saying goes, "Some people are so heavenly minded, they are of no earthly good." This adage certainly fit some members of the church at Corinth. They considered themselves to be spiritually advanced based on the very visible or audible gifts they manifested in worship. But such perceived knowledge often led to behavior that was far less than Christian.

That's because they didn't make the connection between how their physical bodies tied into their service of God. Spirituality was everything to them. And the body? Not so important.

Therefore, they didn't worry about such things as eating meat that had been sacrificed to idols. If their fellow believers were offended or were led into temptation because of it, so what? They even embraced, or at least tolerated, sexually immoral behavior—some of which was so reprehensible that it was not even practiced among pagans (1 Cor. 5:1). But rather than viewing such acts as shameful and worthy of harsh admonition, they rather boasted about their open-mindedness.

While modern-day Christians may not go to some of these unconscionable extremes, many do behave as if the body is of little relevance to our spiritual development and service to God. So Paul's corrective for the Corinthians remains as timely today as in the first century.

Yes, what we do with our bodies does matter. It is a

key part of who we are in Christ.

We Are a Holy Temple (1 Cor. 3:16–17)

Paul, in 1 Corinthians 3, is in the middle of discussing the work that he and Apollos had accomplished in establishing and nurturing the church in Corinth. He reminds his readers that every believer is a builder, and thus should be careful to use quality materials since the work of one's lifetime will be tested by fire. Our time, our talents, our treasures—if we don't press these resources into active service of God and His kingdom, we risk the tragic loss of opportunities that can never be regained.

But again—what is the primary vehicle for putting these valuable gifts into practice? Our functional, physical bodies.

So Paul underlines the importance of this fact by reminding the Corinthians that their bodies are the "temple of God" (3:16). Just as the Old Testament temple was seen as the place of God's habitation on earth, so the new covenant in Christ—personified through His sacrificial death and the subsequent indwelling of His Spirit—means that God now inhabits people, not a building.

Therefore, in its largest sense, this concept of the body as a temple refers to the corporate community of individual believers—the church. This is the context for Paul's strong warning in verse 17, "If any man destroys the temple of God, God will destroy him." He was quite possibly referring to those who wanted to import legalism wholesale into Christianity, proclaiming a false gospel intended to "destroy" the work of grace, leaving no meeting point for holy God and sinful man.

But Paul in chapter 3 is laying the foundation (to be revealed in chapter 6) that the body of each individual believer is also a temple inhabited by the Holy Spirit. For "that is what you are," both corporately and individually—set apart for His service and called to a morally upright life.

Lawful, but Not Profitable (1 Cor. 6:12)

So let's go ahead and jump forward to chapter 6, where matters become a lot more personal. In this section, Paul is dealing specifically with issues of sexual immorality (vv. 15–20), but the principles apply to all aspects concerning the body.

The introductory phrase—"all things are lawful for me" (v. 12)—is very likely a slogan that some in Corinth often said as a way of justifying their conduct. Today, we would put quotation marks around it to indicate that it was being quoted from someone else. Paul actually accepts the basic principle of this statement, but then modifies it based on the implications of the gospel. Since Christians are not saved by works, then yes, we are ultimately free from those things that once held us. But even so, we choose in wisdom to avoid evil and unprofitable things—not because we wish to earn our salvation, but in grateful response to God's redeeming love.

Paul thus makes two important corrections to the arrogant affirmation that "all things are lawful." First, things that may not be expressly forbidden by Scripture should still be avoided if they hinder our effective service to Him. Only those actions that are based on love are expedient to building up the body of Christ, even if technically we could do otherwise.

Second, believers should desire not to be mastered by anything, no matter how permissible the action may be. To paraphrase Paul's words, "All things are under my power, but I will not put myself under the power of anything." It is possible to enslave ourselves to the very behaviors over which we claim to be free. A person might proudly assert his or her freedom to drink alcohol, for example, yet subtly become addicted to it. Another person might feel allowed to eat whatever and whenever they desire, yet over time become unable to control his or her snacking habits. Any kind of behavior that renders us less effective for God's service is sin. Simple as that!

In the first and second century, a significant number of believers argued that nothing done in the body truly mattered to one's spiritual life. Some of them (ascetics) denied all bodily desires, while others (libertines) indulged them. But any practice of Christian faith that ignores the importance of the physical body in serving Christ becomes problematic. We know, for example, that diet and exercise directly impact our vitality and life span, yet we sometimes excuse our eating habits or lack of exercise as if they are unrelated to Christian commitment. We know that emotions such as anxiety and anger can cause a detrimental impact on our health, yet we may ignore them as if they don't impact our Christian walk at all.

Such attitudes run counter to the teaching of the Bible. In striving for physical health, we are seeking first the kingdom.

The Body Is for the Lord (vv. 13–14)

Verse 13 provides us with another apparently well-worn expression of the Corinthians—"Food is for the stomach, and the stomach for food." This saying was perhaps used by the "spirituals" to indicate that the body and everything pertaining to it were inconsequential. The implication (most likely) was not just that eating is a natural function of life, but that one bodily function is basically the same as any other. Therefore, sexual activity is as natural as eating—in which case, fornication is "no big deal." Tragically, this philosophy seems to be the mantra of many today.

Some Corinthians may also have been arguing that since the body is transient, then any sins related to it are therefore insignificant. While it is true, or course, that our earthly bodies in their present forms are only temporary, these bodies of ours will not be destroyed but are destined to be transformed and glorified at the resurrection (1 Cor. 15:35–44; Phil. 3:21). Verse 14 indicates that Paul is thinking along these lines.

So to anyone who says that improper sexual behavior is allowable, Paul doesn't pull any punches: "The body is not for immorality" (v. 13). In fact, he says, the best way to think of the physical self is to say that the body is "for the Lord!" In other words, the body is intended first for the Lord's service (Rom. 6:12–13, 19; 12:21). We could even say that the body of a redeemed person is a gift the Lord has given Himself (1 Cor. 12:18). Furthermore, "the Lord is for the body." He is every bit as necessary to our ability to function as is the sustenance of food, drink, and breathable oxygen. God alone can enable us to live as we were meant to live.

In the following chapters, we will discuss steps you can take to live a healthier, more productive life. Some of these suggestions may seem out of reach. But remember, the Lord is "for" your body—and He desires to empower you to be *Well2Serve*.

Members of Christ (vv. 15–18)

"Do you not know that your bodies are members of Christ?" (v. 15). It is not just that we as grace-bought believers are now members of Christ; our bodies are members of Christ—created and redeemed to serve God. Believers are so closely united to Him that we can be spoken of as being "in Christ" and "members of His body."

This is what makes any sin related to the body so abhorrent.

The most devastating aspect of sin—particularly sexual sin, in this context—is that it "takes away" members of Christ from their proper function. Not only does our sin denigrate that which is holy, but it also deprives God of what is rightfully His. Any sin or addiction that takes you away from your stated purpose of serving God effectively is an affront to His redemptive purpose for your body.

To Paul, the idea of uniting the members of Christ's body with the body of a prostitute is so unspeakable that he concludes his warning against it with a strong repudiation: "May it never be!" (v. 15). For truly, based on the doctrine established in Genesis 2:24—which teaches that sexual union is of such an intimate quality that it spiritually makes two people into one flesh—anyone who sins sexually becomes one body with the other person. How can any believer not see the trouble, even the treachery, in a member of Christ combining his body in this way with someone who is not already joined to him by marriage?

When one places his body at the disposal of another outside of the marriage bond, his body is desecrated, which is a perversion of human nature as God intended it to be. His body has been "taken away" from being used for God's glory to be used instead for his own pleasure. In saying this, Paul does not suggest that sexual immorality is the most serious of all sins. It is not. Yet sexual sin is unique in relation to the body in the sense that it creates an unholy alliance between two people. The believing man thus sins "against his own body" by conducting himself in this way (v. 18) because his body belongs not to a harlot, but to the Lord. We should consider this connection to Him as binding and unbreakable, having a direct bearing on how we choose to behave ourselves physically.

The word "joins" in verse 17—"the one who joins himself to the Lord is one spirit with Him"—literally means "to glue." That's how tightly the spiritual bond between the believer and Christ truly is. And because of this intimate connection, we must make an ongoing habit of fleeing from immorality.

Perhaps, of course, sexual sin may not be an issue for you. But ask yourself: What sin of mine does keep me from being effective in my service to Christ? What takes me away from fruitful activity in His kingdom? Bottom line, you can use your body either to gratify yourself or to glorify God! There are really no other alternatives.

Glorify God in Your Body (vv. 19–20)

Paul, in verse 19, repeats for the sixth time a phrase which indicates he is writing about issues so elementary that his readers should already know them by heart. Here when Paul speaks of the body, he refers to it in the singular, speaking to us as individuals, saying that each Christian is a temple in which God dwells by means of the Holy Spirit. This single assertion gives dignity and majesty to the whole of human life.

Wherever we go and whatever we do, we are bearers of the Holy Spirit. We are the temples in which God has chosen to dwell. This truth rules out all conduct which is not appropriate for the temple of God. Just as we wouldn't deem any and all types of behavior to be appropriate for the church sanctuary, we should implement the same kind of discretion in what we tolerate for our own bodies—which, in real terms, are more legitimately the temple of God than even the church building.

And lest we think this principle only implies to matters like fornication—no, it also concerns the careless, derogatory manner in which we may treat our bodies in terms of a greasy diet, lazy habits, and a failure to seek healthy balance and rest.

"You are not your own," Paul says (v. 19). This statement stands in stark contrast to many of our assertions and attitudes that say my body belongs to me and I can do with it whatever I please. Quite the opposite, we are no longer the proprietors of our own bodies, because we have been "bought with a price" (v. 20)— an exorbitant price—purchased by God through the death of His Son.

When man attempted to gain freedom from His Creator, he became a slave to sin. Yet ironically, the only way he can now become free is by becoming what he was intended to be—a son and servant of the Creator, the One who owns him from fingertip to fingertip.

In this way, the obligation to glorify God in our bodies becomes the true motivation for the way we conduct our lives—in our eating and exercising, as well as in our physical maintenance and moral behavior. Being *Well2Serve* is not simply about looking better at the beach. The care of our body is about Him, not us. Since our body is His temple, we must use it for His glory.

For Memory and Meditation

"Do you not know that your body is a temple of the Holy Spirit who is in you, whom you have from God, and that you are not your own?" (1 Cor. 6:19).

WELL*FACTS*

Make fitness doable: Dream big, discover what moves you, set and record goals, mix it up, and find a buddy. Warren, 149.

More than half of people surveyed find it easier to figure out their income taxes than to know how to eat right. Rath, 1.

Sitting is the most underrated health threat of modern times. This subtle epedemic is eroding our health. On a global level, inactivity now kills more people than smoking. Rath, 21.

A very important question to ask yourself is this: "Is the way I'm living and feeling now the way I want to live and feel five years from now? Ten years from now? Twenty years from now? Reynolds, 35.

Christians should be the most healthy people group, especially when we consider the physical condition of Jesus Christ, our Founder and leader. Reynolds, 21.

God created our bodies, and He created them for himself. Your body is the temple of the Holy Spirit. Reynolds, 35.

Medical research is showing more and more that there may be a mind-body connection to most diseases and ailments, not just a few. Colbert, 25.

WELL*ACTS*

The redeemed body is a gift God gives to Himself. What are the implications of the biblical truth expressed by the statement, "Your body is not your own"?

Our connection to Christ makes sins of the body abhorrent. What destructive habits have you allowed to master you?

What excuses are you making for destructive behavior?

Which particular bodily sins are keeping you from effective service?

Begin with a prayer of confession which comes from your response to the questions above. Ask the Lord to forgive your sins and to cleanse you from all unrighteousness. Claim and celebrate that forgiveness.

Get a step counter. Set a goal to get 10,000 steps a day.

Continue to journal your progress as you present your entire being to God. Repent for the failures and celebrate the victories as you continue on your wellness journey.

Are you meeting regular with your accountability partners? Remember the power of a team.

Your Body: Earthly Instrument for Service

CHAPTER 5

Focal Text: Romans 12:1–2

As a child, one of my favorite Christmas songs was The Little Drummer Boy. It not only had a catchy little tune, but its lyrics were extremely hopeful and encouraging. The little boy, as you recall, didn't believe he could bring anything of value as a gift to the King. All he knew how to do was to play his little drum. He discovered, however, that bringing his best before the King was an appropriate gift all by itself.

Do you ever feel like the little drummer boy, wondering if you have anything of value to present to the King? I think many Christians fail to serve Him with freedom and consistency because they somehow imagine they have nothing worthy to present to Him. If this sentiment strikes a familiar chord in your heart, I hope the implications of today's lesson will get you marching to a different beat. Believe in your uniqueness!

The Mercies of God

In the letter to the Romans, the division between theological teaching (chaps. 1–11) and practical application (12–15) is more pronounced than in many of the Pauline letters. Nonetheless, the practical instructions found in the latter part of the book are both related to and dependent upon the theological foundation laid out in the first eleven chapters. Right at the conjunction point where these two massive pieces of Biblical literature come together is the transitional phrase that begins chapter 12— "Therefore, I urge you, brethren, by the mercies of God . . ."

In several places throughout the early chapters of Romans, Paul graphically describes man's sin problem—the universality of our fallenness (3:23) and the rightful punishment of death for our disobedience (6:23). But through the "mercies of God," He has chosen to justify those who believe in Christ by faith, thus allowing us to have peace with Him (5:1).

This declaration of our new standing before Him— dead to sin and alive to Christ—comes with profound implications, not only for our eternal salvation, but also for our physical bodies. As Romans 6:13 declares, "Do not go on presenting the members of your body to sin as instruments of unrighteousness; but present yourselves to God as those alive from the dead, and your members as instruments of righteousness to God."

Our bodies are powerful instruments. They bear the potential for great evil or great good. Paul says that when we give our bodies to sin, we become a slave of that particular behavior, resulting in bondage and death (6:16). But because of God's mercies, we who were formerly slaves to these appetites and desires can become obedient to God and thus instruments of righteousness. Your body is the instrument God designed for effective service to Him as He advances His kingdom on earth through you. How exciting is that?

Through His mercy, even our flawed and limited physical bodies can become tools that He sends into action at His good pleasure and will. And none of us wants to be found unready for such valuable assignments.

Present Your Body to God

We've looked at Romans 12 previously. But today, just as you might dig a little deeper inside yourself, looking for the energy to run one more lap or do ten more crunches, we take our study to a new level, discovering even richer truths as we pull them to the surface.

The last phrase of verse 1, as we've said, characterizes the presentation of our bodies to God as our "spiritual" or "reasonable" act of worship. The Greek word is logikos, which brings to our ears the idea of this being a logical, sensible response based on what God has done for us. But Paul doesn't leave it to his readers to figure this out on their own. He "urges" them to think of themselves as a living sacrifice. The word translated "urge" was used in classical Greek as a means of exhorting troops into battle. In Paul's case, it represents the weight of his apostolic authority. He means business. He's expecting people to follow his lead.

And as we do so, the Scripture says, make no mistake: this is worship. The presentation of our bodies to God is every bit as much of a worship service as what you and I do in church on Sunday mornings. Through the death of His Son, He has made us alive with Him (Rom. 6:4–6), and the offering of our bodies is one way we express our thanks. It's worship.

Paul's mention of "living sacrifice" would have made this point very clear to his original readers. Such language obviously brings to mind the sacrificial system of the Old Testament. But in contrast to "dead animal" sacrifices, Christians are to present their bodies as living sacrifices. When you think of it, what else could we offer to God than the body He has made alive? We who have received mercy are now empowered to express that mercy through bodies that have been quickened by the power of the resurrection and made capable by the gifts of His Spirit.

For as we've seen, this is the real purpose of our bodies: to engage in the ministry of spiritual gifts, as Paul discusses in verses 3–8. These gifts are given to every believer for effective service of the King. Spiritual gifts are never a "premium upgrade," available only to a select few members of the community. No, they are part and parcel of the life of grace. But in order for their true meaning to come to life, we must present them back to the King for His service and glory.

The remainder of chapter 12—in both the beauty and practicality of its teaching—stems from this opening appeal to bring our bodies before God as a living sacrifice. When we do, a whole world of spiritual worship and ministry begins to flow from it.

Living, Holy, and Acceptable

These three qualifying words in verse 1—"living," "holy," and "acceptable"—are of equal value, and thus together they define what is involved in the presentation of our bodies.

Living not only provides a contrast with dead animal sacrifices but has a broader theological meaning. As believers, we have been raised from the dead and granted newness of life (Rom. 6:4), so our bodies now have the potential of producing righteous acts for God. This word also signifies that the offering of our bodies is a daily and ongoing gift to Him. Further, this gift of ourselves can be called "living" because it has the potential to give life to others as it points them to Christ.

Holy is a word that underlines both the totality of our sacrifice and its ethical character. The word translated as the verb "to present" is a technical term for the offering of a sacrifice, literally meaning "to place beside." Thus as Christians, our bodies are separated totally to the Lord to use as He desires. This means we no longer make claims on how or when we are willing to serve Him. In addition, our sacrifice is "holy" in an ethical sense, because God who indwells and empowers us by the person of the Holy Spirit is holy. Our gifted service to the King should be such that it reveals the holiness of God, bringing glory to Him and not to ourselves as the gifted servant.

Acceptable describes the presentation of our bodies as being all that God requires. Anything less is inappropriate and insufficient—unacceptable. He prizes the full offering of ourselves, no matter how little we may deem its worth. The way we hamper the advance of God's kingdom is not by our lack of ability, but by placing conditions of time and convenience on our service to Him, offering Him less than our best.

He made you for Himself, redeemed you by His grace, and gifted you by His Spirit to serve alongside Him in the earthly advance of His kingdom. No matter what your area of gifted service, God accepts it with fatherly pleasure and pride.

My nine grandchildren are the joy of my life. They

often present their "Papa" with pictures they have drawn. I can't always readily discern what their scribbling was meant to capture, but these drawings still bring me great pleasure, and I quickly and proudly display them on my refrigerator door. I humorously like to think of God as having a refrigerator door like mine, except as big as all of heaven, on which He displays our gifted service to Him. Our childlike "drawings" may only represent our fumbling attempt to present the gospel to someone or sing a solo that sounded like a disaster. But to His eyes and ears, our gifts have already been declared "acceptable."

Get out your crayons and start drawing for the King!

Renewing of the Mind

Just as the presentation of our bodies is an "urgent" need in making us effective servants of the King, so too is the daily renewing of our minds (v. 2). These are the twin pillars upon which the exercise of our giftedness is constructed.

Christian service takes place in the real world, against real temptations, operating in places where confusion and insecurity are always easy to come by. Therefore, we must guard ourselves against being conformed to the values of the present age. We are daily bombarded with messages telling us that our life is really all about us—which suggests that financial attainment, power, physical looks, and awards are the true measures of greatness. We are easily tempted to buy into this false value system, allowing the world to squeeze us into its mold.

The only solution to this constant pressure is to be "transformed by the renewing of your mind."

As kingdom citizens desiring to live according to our created purpose, we know that this present world order is already in the process of dissolution and will be destroyed by the return of the rightful King. "Therefore, since we receive a kingdom which cannot be shaken, let us show gratitude, by which we may offer to God an acceptable service with reverence and awe" (Heb. 12:28). Let us offer up to Him our thoughts, beliefs, observations, and presuppositions to be shaped by His Word and His Spirit so that we can enter each day transformed.

The thought of continual transformation permeates Paul's teaching in the Roman letter. "Therefore do not let sin reign in your mortal body," he says, "but present yourselves to God as those alive from the dead, and your members as instruments of righteousness to God" (6:12–13). Understanding our true identity in Christ and the kingdom potential provided to us through redemption can ignite our passion to serve the King. Many Christians stop halfway. They are made alive through grace, but rarely if submit themselves to God for service. This lack of kingdom initiative and availability allows them to be sucked back into the tyrannizing power of the flesh and the world.

The issue here is our entire thinking process—our worldview. The world says that life is about me; thus I pursue those things which promote my own kingdom. The transformed mind, however, views the world from the standpoint of God's kingdom and our role in it. I start with the question of "How can I advance God's kingdom?" And by following that trail to its logical end, I begin to fulfill my created purpose, experience radical freedom in Christ, and discover a life of real meaning, joy, and contentment—the very opposite result of an egocentric worldview.

In Romans 8, Paul pays particular attention to the transforming work of the Spirit and the role of the mind in transformation. "For those who are according to the flesh set their minds on the things of the flesh, but those who are according to the Spirit, the things of the Spirit. For the mind set on the flesh is death, but the mind set on the Spirit is life and peace (vv. 5–6). We see, then, that this transformation of the mind is not really an issue of becoming more intelligent. It is a reorientation of both thought and deed to align with the truth.

The "mind" in Scripture denotes the inner part of the human constitution, the place where feeling, thinking, and willing takes place. The non-Christian's, reprobate mind leads that person into a futile lifestyle. "Just as they did not see fit to acknowledge God any longer, God gave them over to a depraved mind, to do those things which are not proper" (Rom. 1:28). The believer's mind, on the other hand—made alive through spiritual conversion—can be constantly renewed, enabling us to "prove the will of God" (Rom. 12:2).

The word "prove" here is not just a mental, judicial, theoretical term. It means to know and to do—to understand God's will and to live it out. And that's exactly what God invites you to experience more and more—the living proof of what He says about you in His Word and what He can achieve in your heart, in your body, in your mind, throughout the totality of your person-hood. That's what it means to be *Well2Serve*.

We are not talking here about the "power of positive thinking"—the false promise that what your mind can conceive, your life can achieve. My mind may tell me that I can hit a 300-yard tee shot like those guys on the PGA Tour—but that is not going to happen. By renewing my mind, however, God does enable me to see myself from His perspective. I can see that my gifts are living, holy, and acceptable to Him. I can see my life through the lens of grace and discern the working of the Holy Spirit in me.

He will provide us the supernatural resources needed to serve Him effectively as we present Him our bodies, as we let Him transform our minds.

For Memory and Meditation

"Do not be conformed to this world, but be transformed by the renewing of your mind, so that you may prove what the will of God is, that which is good and acceptable and perfect" (Rom. 12:2).

After all, living longer shouldn't be about "taking longer to die.". . . It should be about enjoying every moment of a longer life—and taking longer to live. Roizen, 16.

Practicing a behavior, such as saying no to the doughnuts, actually strengthens the willpower circuits in the brain. Amen, Kindle, 2997.

Scientific research has found that physical activity can cut cravings whether you crave sugary snacks or things like cigarettes, alcohol, or drugs. Amen, Kindle, 3001.

At the Amen Clinics, we performed a SPECT study, which found that practicing gratitude causes real changes in your brain that enhance brain function and make you feel better. Amen, Kindle, 3493.

For example, a major study, also published in Circulation, found that regular exercise worked even better than angioplasty for preventing heart attacks, strokes, and premature deaths. Ornish, 18.

We too often think that the physical reality determines the unseen reality of the soul, mind, and emotions. The Bible tells us the exact opposite process is in effect. The unseen reality of our souls, minds, and emotions is what determines the physical reality we perceive with our senses. Colbert, 46

Are there areas of your thinking that are being conformed to the world? If so, list them in your journal and ask God to cleanse these from your mind.

Participate in the process of the renewal of your mind by viewing yourself from God's perspective. "I am created by His hand, redeemed by His grace, gifted and empowered by His Spirit, chosen to be His co-laborer in kingdom service!" Commit this affirmation to memory and repeat it each morning before you get out of bed.

Have you ever presented yourself to God as a living sacrifice? Just as it is necessary to confess with the mouth your commitment to follow Christ (Rom. 10:9–10), it is also important to confess your willingness to be a living sacrifice. Pray this prayer—"Father, today I present my body to you. You have gifted me and empowered me to serve You, and that is my heart's desire. Use me anywhere and anytime You choose. Amen." Journal your thoughts on this commitment.

Can you identify your spiritual gift(s)? If not, ask God to show you what He created you to do in service to Him. Second, ask a spiritually mature friend what they believe your gift might be. Third, just try several areas of service and ask God to give you affirmation when you are serving in your gifted area. Believe that you are God's unique instrument!

Nourish the Body

CHAPTER 6

Focal Texts: Leviticus 11:1–3, 44–45; Daniel 1:11–16

"You are what you eat!"

"If you don't finish your vegetables, you can't have dessert!"

Remember those? Some of these quaint sayings may have been helpful in the development of good eating habits. But others—such as, "Clean your plate before you leave the table"—may have actually encouraged overeating, which has now become a significant health concern. In a country obsessed with "biggie sizing" everything, we are facing a crisis of obesity today which impacts us physically, mentally, and spiritually.

"Nearly one-half of the American population will be obese by 2030 according to a 2012 study published by the American Journal of Preventive Medicine. The researchers estimate that this will result in an additional $66 billion dollars in health care expenditures, 7.8 million new cases of stroke and heart disease, and 539.000 new cancer diagnoses."[1]

We all are accustomed to hearing such reports these days. But this is not simply a health issue. For believers, it is chiefly an issue of effective kingdom service.

We have already spoken of redemption as an experience that takes in the entirety of who we are—heart, soul, mind, and body. We have also seen that the body is the temple of the Holy Spirit, the primary instrument

[1] Scott Stoll, *Fat in Church*, FoxNews.com, Jan. 04, 2013.

for worship. It therefore stands to reason that we must take care of these bodies so we can present them to God as an acceptable sacrifice.

And that means watching what we put in our mouths. Proper nourishment is a critical part of temple maintenance.

The Calling to Priestly Status (Exod. 19:5–6)

Instead of beginning this study in a customary place, let's travel back to Exodus 19, where God has just delivered Israel from Egyptian bondage. Moses has led Israel out of captivity and to the base of Mount Sinai to meet with God. God there instructs Moses to tell the Israelites that they have been redeemed with missional purpose. He speaks not only of delivering them from the Egyptians, but also of bringing them to Himself (v. 4), where through His covenant He has made them His own unique possession, a kingdom of priests, and a holy nation (vv. 5–6).

This word that describes the people of God as His "possession" carries the idea of being "moveable"— indicating that they are to move at His command, to serve Him in any and every context of life He chooses for them. Further, as a "kingdom of priests," they are to represent Him on earth. And to represent a holy God, they themselves must be "holy."

God was seeking a people who would embody His character, embrace His mission, and obey His word— and to live this way "among all the peoples" (v. 5). Israel was to represent God wherever they were placed, among whomever they found themselves.

But why? Why such an extreme and total demand?

Because, He says, "all the earth is Mine" (v. 5). This is not simply an affirmation that God created everything; it is a statement of mission. Recall mankind's attempt in Genesis 11 to live a self-dependent life without God, signified by the ambitious tower of Babel. They said, "Come, let us build for ourselves a city, and a tower whose top will reach into heaven, and let us make for ourselves a name, otherwise we will be scattered abroad over the face of the whole earth" (v. 4). And that's exactly what God did—scattering the nations and confusing their languages. But far from being a mere act of divine judgment, it was an act of surprising love, preventing them from a life devoid of the One True God. And ever since, God has been actively seeking to work through a "called people" to bring all nations back under His kingly rule. This is our mission as His moveable priests on earth.

But such a mission requires physical strength. Well nourished bodies. No wonder, then, that among the regulations and procedures found in Leviticus—those preparations that enabled Israel to represent holy God to a pagan culture—we find a set of principles that relate particularly to the nourishment of the physical body.

Consecrate Yourselves (Lev. 11:44–45)

It may be a bit unusual to study a passage by beginning at the end, but I believe we are warranted to do so in Leviticus 11, because the latter verses articulate the basis for the strict dietary laws that precede them. The phrase, "be holy, for I am holy," is like a refrain which plays throughout the entire book, and is spoken twice within these two verses. Man's highest duty is to worship and imitate his Creator. So if Israel was to represent a holy God, they must be a distinctive people in every aspect of their lives.

No issue of our daily existence is too small to be submitted to the will of God. If the various minutia we find in Leviticus communicate anything to our modern ears, it is this: all of our earthly existence comes within God's purview. Paul restated this principle clearly in 1 Corinthians 10:31: "Whether, then, you eat or drink or whatever you do, do all to the glory of God."

So like the priestly generation of old, we as His modern day priestly people (1 Pet. 2:5–9) must "consecrate" ourselves, must "become holy." Sanctified. Completely set apart. This calls for more than periodic church attendance and occasional prayer. It demands constant effort and spiritual discipline. To be holy requires that we submit our total selves to Him and to His control, including our physical appetites and eating habits.

We have often been guilty of disconnecting our following of Christ from the stewardship of the body—our nourishment, our movement, our rest, and our thinking. But God's people must be entirely surrendered to Him, distinctive in every area of life. We must seek to live free of any evil pollution of body, mind, or spirit.

Why Such an Emphasis on Food? (Lev. 11:1–3)

Since food is necessary for human survival, we would naturally expect God to give His people instructions concerning this fundamental part of man's existence. And here is how He primarily does it in Leviticus—by focusing on foods that would make a person "unclean."

The idea of being "unclean," of course, went far beyond food. A person could become unclean in other ways, such as by giving birth, touching a dead body, or having certain skin conditions. So, obviously, not everything that rendered a person unclean was deliberately sinful. And yet anything that made someone unclean would disqualify them—at least temporarily—from participating in certain worship events. This is why God wanted every individual to be "clean," enabling them to offer service to God. He desires that we be *Well2Serve*.

Leviticus 11 begins: "The Lord spoke again to Moses and to Aaron . . ." (v. 1). This issue of clean and unclean food was not a matter of folk wisdom, passed down through the generations—such as the way certain dietary codes can be developed within cultures today. I recall my dad, for example, holding a revival meeting at my little seminary church in Wolf Creek, North Carolina. The men there were very adept at harvesting mushrooms in the forest. And at one of our evening meals that week, we were presented with a generous helping of fried mushrooms. Dad, who was never a picky eater, seemed a bit reluctant to partake. He finally broke the awkward silence by asking how a person could tell edible mushrooms from the poisonous kind. Our host simply replied, "You eat 'em, and if they don't kill you, then they're good." This is obviously not the way Israel compiled their list of unclean animals. Their instructions were given by God Himself.

Actually, the idea of clean and unclean animals already existed at this time, having originated before the flood. We find a mention of clean animals in the instructions Noah was given concerning how many of each creature was to be taken aboard the ark (Genesis 7:2–3, 8–9). Clean animals were not taken in pairs but in groupings of seven. And not only could they be eaten by Noah and his family but could also be offered as a sacrifice after the flood (8:20). Here again the issue is sacrificial service to the Lord.

It is also instructive to note that Leviticus 11 begins with positive permission, not simply prohibition. "These are the creatures which you may eat from all the animals that are on the earth" (v. 2). God is not just trying to spoil our enjoyment, as if saying that anything that tastes good is obviously bad for you. His will and desire is to actively, purposefully provide for man's physical nourishment.

Various suggestions have been made as to why certain animals were deemed unclean. Each theory contains both validity and drawbacks. But the best and simplest solution is that these dietary restrictions simply reflected God's desire for Israel to be a holy nation, unique among all others, serving as a witness to the nations around them. Should this seem so odd? Isn't adherence to a particular diet often associated with religious commitment? As a child, for instance, I knew nothing about the Catholic faith, except that fish was always on the school lunch menu on Fridays. This one conviction told me something about what they represented.

Note also that the foods considered clean were the

same as those that could be offered to God as a sacrifice (Gen. 7:8–9). Since the person making an offering would often partake of the food himself in the worship celebration, any food deemed appropriate for God would also need to be appropriate for the worshiper.

Deuteronomy 14: 2 stands as a good summary statement: "For you are a holy people to the Lord your God, and the Lord has chosen you to be a people for His own possession out of all the peoples who are on the face of the earth." We can conclude that diet—like everything else—is related to our worship, our service, and our witness.

The Witness of Daniel (Dan. 1:11–17)

The story of Daniel and his three friends provides a great illustration of diet serving as a witness of one's commitment to God. Israel had been taken into Babylonian captivity. Nebuchadnezzar, the Babylonian king, ordered that some of the outstanding youth of Israel be brought into the palace for a three-year training program to equip them to serve in the king's court. They were to be taught the literature and language of the Chaldeans and be fed from the king's table (vv. 3–5). This food would certainly have been rich, high quality fare, and the Babylonians would have been convinced that nothing surpassed it in ensuring a person's good health. Daniel, however, made up his mind that he would not defile himself with the king's food or wine, and requested instead a ten-day diet consisting of vegetables and water (vv. 8–13).

In the end, Daniel's diet did cause the Israelite youths to appear visibly healthier than those who partook of the king's food (vv. 15–16), and God's hand gave these young men favor (v. 17)—not only in their physical strength but in every area of life, such that they were seen to be head and shoulders above others in the land (cf. 1:20).

We may wonder why the king's food would have caused Daniel concern. It is likely that some of the meats that the Babylonians served were among those listed as "unclean" in Leviticus 11. Further, he may have felt he was compromising God's standards to eat food that had been consecrated by a pagan prayer. Or—most likely of all—he simply perceived that the entire process of palace living and a rich diet was designed to seduce him into a life-style of Babylonian pleasure, which would blunt his total commitment to God. The "good life" the king offered was designed to wean him from the "hard life" to which God had called him. It could lead him to think of himself as a distinguished courtier rather than a servile Israelite.[2]

For any or all of these reasons, Daniel's commitment to serve the King of kings rather than the king of Babylon enabled him to bear an effective witness in a pagan culture, declaring his uniqueness as one chosen to serve God with his entire being.

Modern-Day Reflections

This chapter is not intended to promote a particular diet, such as the vegetarian one that Daniel chose. The word translated "vegetables," by the way, refers to that which grows from seeds; thus, Daniel's diet could

---

[2] See Sinclair B. Ferguson, *Daniel* in *The Communicator's Commentary*. Word Books: Waco, Texas, 1988), pp.35-36.

have consisted not only of vegetables, but also fruit, grains, and bread. Nor should we conclude that Daniel considered all meat forbidden, for it was indeed allowed in the Israelites' diet—even commanded on the Passover.

The point is simply to affirm that even our diet is of great concern to God and is intricately related to our overall health, which in turn impacts our ability to serve Him. Our bodies are temples of the Holy Spirit, and eating (or overeating) from a poor diet is a way of destroying what God has given us. To not obey Him in this way is poor stewardship on several levels—impacting our strength and stamina, while negatively affecting our service to Him and presenting a bad witness to the world. Additionally, it consumes resources which could be shared with those who have little or no access to an adequate diet.

Memorize and mediate on our verse for the week, and ask God to guide you as you nourish your body.

For Memory and Meditation

"Whether, then, you eat or drink or whatever you do, do all to the glory of God" (1 Cor. 10:31).

WELL*FACTS*

A study of 80,000+ people suggests that total intake of fruits and vegetables is a robust predictor of overall happiness. Rath, 29.

For example, one study published in the Journal of the American Medical Association (JAMA) found that those who are 30 pounds overweight lose between one and six years of life, while those who are about 100 pounds overweight lose up to 13 years of life. Finkelstein, Kindle 235.

Religious involvement is linked to many positive health outcomes, such as happiness, lower rates of smoking and alcohol use, and even a longer life. But research has also suggested that middle-aged adults who are more religious are more likely to be obese. Park, Kindle, 2011.

Restricting calories, increasing your strength, and getting quality sleep are three of nature's best anti-aging medicines. Roizen, 15.

Food has the power to heal us. It is the most potent tool we have to prevent and treat many of our chronic diseases—including diabetes and obesity. Warren, 76.

WELL*ACTS*

Cut your calorie intake by eating smaller portions.

Increase your intake of healthy omega-3 fatty acids by eating fish like salmon and mahi-mahi. Aim for 13 ounces a week.

Greatly restrict or cut out altogether refined sugars.

Eat as much vegetables and fruit as you like. Make sure you have two or more portions of vegetables a day. Many of them contain powerful antioxidants. Eat at least 3 or more vegetables and 2 fruits daily.

Nuts are a good source of protein and thus make a healthy snack food.

Olive oil—the "extra virgin" kind—contains healthy fats that can help extend your life.

Switch to whole grain breads.

Looking for a sweet snack? Dark chocolate actually lowers blood pressure.

Talk to your doctor before starting any specific diet program.

Drink 8-10 glasses of pure water a day.

Move the Body

Focal Text: 1 Corinthians 9:24–27

I was privileged to grow up in a preacher's home, and quickly learned that ministry was no church picnic. It is hard work. Not only does it require long, sometimes exhausting hours, it also involves numerous situations which are emotionally draining. When I saw this happening in my dad, I realized that his day and duties could be as physically taxing as some of my football practices.

My mom, too, was a ministry partner, and I observed from her life that even the service rendered by laypersons can be as physically demanding as that of professional, full-time ministers. My older sister and brother, in the years since, have always been actively involved in ministry and leadership positions in their churches, and I went on to follow in my dad's footsteps. So I can affirm from much personal, up close experience the essential need for being *Well2Serve.*

I have written and spoken about church health for several decades now, and the one constant concern I hear is what is often known as the 80/20 rule—twenty percent of people doing eighty percent of the work. In conference after conference, staff and laypersons alike echo the concern that people today are unwilling to serve. I am beginning to wonder, though, if this lack of service from the 80 percent is as much a physical problem as a spiritual one. If people are always worn out, maxed out, and stressed out, they don't have the energy to add anything else to their schedules.

They are just too tired to serve.

Do you think the apostle Paul could relate to this fatigue factor? I have always admired his life and have looked to him as a model for ministry. In 2 Corinthians, he speaks very candidly about the challenges he faced: imprisonments, beatings, frequent journeys, many dangers and difficulties. "I have been in labor and hardship," he says, "through many sleepless nights, in hunger and thirst, often without food, in cold and exposure. Apart from such external things, there is the daily pressure on me of concern for all the churches" (2 Cor. 11:27–28).

So he obviously understood the demands on anyone who is serious about serving Christ to the full extent of his or her time and ability. But how did he cope? How did he keep up his rigorous ministry schedule? And how did he both counsel and encourage those who were active along with him in kingdom service?

Paul's Testimony

Paul frequently speaks of the hard labor involved in serving Christ. In writing to the Thessalonians, for example, he describes his recent ministry in a nearby city: "But after we had already suffered and been mistreated in Philippi, as you know, we had boldness in our God to speak to you the gospel of God amid much opposition" (1 Thess. 2:2).

In Colossians, he repeatedly mentions the endurance required in ministry. Speaking about his goal to present every believer complete before God, he says, "For this purpose also I labor, striving according to His power, which mightily works within me. For I want you to know how great a struggle I have on your behalf and for those who are at Laodicea" (Col. 1:29–2:1).

The word translated "labor" (kopiao) in this passage means "to work to exhaustion"—the same word used in 1 Thessalonians 5:12 to describe the diligent work of those in pastoral leadership. "Striving" contains the imagery of exerting maximum effort in an athletic event—a term from which we derive the English word "agony." "Struggle" is another athletic word, describing a contest which is strenuous and demanding.

But of all the athletic images he employs, the idea of "running a race" is the most frequent. In his farewell address to church leaders in Ephesus, recorded in Acts 20, he declares, "But I do not consider my life of any account as dear to myself, so that I may finish my course and the ministry which I received from the Lord Jesus, to testify solemnly of the gospel of the grace of God" (v. 24). Finishing the race was a key driver in his desire to stay physically strong.

In Galatians 2:2, Paul describes his trip to Jerusalem to ensure the accuracy of the gospel he was preaching to the Gentiles. His concern is that he "might be running, or had run, in vain." Philippians 2:16 uses the same athletic imagery, yet this time with great confidence that his strenuous labor has not been for nothing. He speaks of "holding fast the word of life, so that in the day of Christ I will have reason to glory because I did not run in vain nor toil in vain." (The word translated "toil," by the way, is the Greek kopiao, which we have already seen on two occasions.) The imagery is clear. Paul is like a cross-country runner in his quest to spread the gospel, unwilling to let his own self-interest—or even the preservation of his own life—impede him in his race to faithfully serve God (v. 17).

In 2 Timothy, Paul uses the imagery of a soldier, an athlete, and a hardworking farmer to encourage Timothy to stand strong in his service to the Lord. "Suffer hardship with me, as a good soldier of Christ Jesus. No soldier in active service entangles himself in the affairs of everyday life, so that he may please the one who enlisted him as a soldier. Also if anyone competes as an athlete, he does not win the prize unless he competes according to the rules. The hardworking farmer ought to be the first to receive his share of the crops" (2:3–6). The soldier avoids distractions to please his commander; the athlete competes by the rules to win the prize; and the industrious farmer works to enjoy the fruit of his labor.

So without a doubt—from Paul's testimony alone, if not from our own firsthand knowledge—service in the spiritual realm is hard work. It demands that we present to God an instrument (our body) which is physically fit, able to endure the rigors that our individual tasks require.

What if you knew, then, that you could very likely extend your potential years of service to the King through something as simple as an exercise program? Would you do it? Would it be worth the extra effort?

The Pauline Formula (1 Cor. 9:24–27)

Paul provides us with a useful four-step program that can guide our thinking—and steel our perseverance—as we seek to offer God our very best in every area of our lives, including the development of our physical strength and stamina. Paul's coaching tips (found in 1 Corinthians 9) come within the context of discussing his "rights" as a man with apostolic credentials, one whose enormous investment in the churches he served entitled him to compensation for his tireless efforts.

But he declares himself willing to forgo whatever return he should reasonably expect, because his bottom line for ministry (as summarized in verse 23) is that "I do all things for the sake of the gospel, so that I may become a fellow partaker of it." His true motivation behind the spiritual and physical discipline he exerted so tirelessly was not to earn well deserved payment but to maximize the great privilege accorded him to live out and declare the gospel.

So as we, too, think about matters of diet and exercise, let's not disconnect them from our calling and desire to serve God with our whole being. Let's follow Paul's inspiring advice, which says:

1. Always run to win (v. 24). The Corinthians would have been familiar with the rules of athletic contests, since the Isthmian games (second only to the Olympics) were held in Corinth every two years. During any of the running events—as anyone knows—only one competitor can take first prize. But if dedicated athletes are willing to train with such diligence, knowing that only one runner can be crowned champion, shouldn't the Christian strive with equal diligence to be effective in the King's service, knowing that a crown of blessing awaits every participant?

Paul, for his part, didn't want anything impeding

his progress toward that goal—even the well deserved rights of an apostle. And neither should we want anything impeding us as we strive to serve our God for His glory. Not all people would categorize a lack of physical fitness as sinful—any more than Paul's claim to personal recognition was sinful. But if it restricts us from being at peak availability for Christ, do we not sin against Him by not doing what is within our power to build our strength? We need to think of physical exercise as "temple conditioning" that enables us to run a winning race for Christ.

2. Exercise self-control (v. 25). Paul again employs the Greek word from which we get the English "agony." Halfhearted effort is never enough from an athlete who truly wants to win. Every competitor in the Isthmian games underwent strict training for ten months to qualify for participation, exercising self-control "in all things," merely to win a "perishable wreath." We know of many modern day athletes who make great sacrifices for the privilege of representing their country, denying themselves lawful pleasures to be at their competitive best.

Does their strenuous self-denial not deliver a strong rebuke to the halfhearted, flabby Christian who claims to be a fully devoted follower of Christ? After all, we are not competing for a worldly prize but for the pleasure of our King—an imperishable reward from our Father in heaven.[3]

3. Take clear aim (v. 26). Runners in the Isthmian games had a clear destination in mind—the finish

[3] If you want to study more about your reward in heaven, you would enjoy the 12 week study by Ken Hemphill titled *Live It Up*. Look at Auxanopress for information concerning the materials for this study.

line—and they were unwilling to take any path or approach that deviated from that goal. Boxing contestants, as well, would never be content with just wildly "beating the air." They wanted every blow to hit its intended target. This image could refer to shadow boxing or to actually missing an opponent with a punch. But boxers do not want to expend any energy that doesn't bring results.

Have you established clear aims for your spiritual service? What do you want to accomplish for God with the life He has given you? Are you serving in such a way that every dimension of your life is focused on accomplishing that goal?

4. Discipline the body (v. 27). Paul may still be using the imagery created by the boxer mentioned in verse 26. The word translated "discipline" or "buffet" is from a Greek word that can mean "to beat black and blue." Paul insists that he has made his body his slave for the sake of the gospel. The picture is that of an athlete who keeps his body under control so that it will serve him well in achieving his set goal—winning the race, dominating the match. Paul wants to be sure that nothing he does—from lack of desire, lack of effort, or lack of anything which he can attain in his body through devoted discipline—is able to make him ineffective in his work.

By using the terminology of being "disqualified," Paul is not suggesting that he could be in danger of losing his salvation. But in sports, a participant who is disqualified must forfeit his prize. And in our service to God, disqualification could involve the loss of opportunity and readiness, not having the right punch at the right time.

This same idea is found in 1 Corinthians 3:15, where Paul is encouraging each person to build on the foundation of Christ with gold, silver, and precious stones, not with wood, hay, or straw. The quality of each man's work will one day be tested, and whatever amount of it remains will procure for him a reward. "If any man's work is burned up, he will suffer loss; but he himself will be saved, yet so as through fire." Everything God has given us in this life—time, talents, treasures, our bodies—comes with kingdom potential. And if what we do in and through this body is of a golden quality, our reward will be to lay it down before His feet in heaven as a prized offering to Him.

The reason we are willing to discipline our bodies has nothing to do with impressing others, but everything to do with pleasing our Lord, doing everything possible to maintain our fitness until the Lord's return.

The Great Cloud of Witnesses (Heb. 12:1–2)

Surely one of the most famous sports images in the Bible is the one found in Hebrews 12:1. "Therefore, since we have so great a cloud of witnesses surrounding us, let us also lay aside every encumbrance and the sin which so easily entangles us, and let us run with endurance the race that is set before us, fixing our eyes on Jesus, the author and perfecter of faith, who for the joy set before Him endured the cross, despising the shame, and has sat down at the right hand of the throne of God."

When we think of those who are now witnessing our race—more importantly, the one who endured the cross for us—we should be moved to lay aside every encumbrance so that we can run with endurance. And if one of those encumbrances is overeating or laziness or an avoidance of regular exercise, remember that we are competing for an imperishable reward. And no cost is too high.

Here is a great promise to claim. Memorize this verse and mediate on it daily.

For Memory and Meditation

"I have fought the good fight, I have finished the course, I have kept the faith; in the future there is laid up for me the crown of righteousness, which the Lord, the righteous Judge, will award to me on that day; and not only to me, but also to all who have loved His appearing" (2 Tim. 4:7).

WELL*FACTS*

On a global level, inactivity now kills more people than smoking. Rath, Kindle, 343.

Sitting more than six hours a day greatly increases your risk of an early death. Rath, Kindle, 346.

A 2012 study in the journal PLOS Medicine showed that 2.5 hours of moderate exercise per week (that's half an hour of brisk walking a day for 5 days) increased life expectancy by 3.5 years. Metzl, 3.

Low fitness stood out by far as the single strongest predictor of death—more powerful even than obesity, diabetes, high cholesterol, high blood pressure, and smoking. Metzl, 12.

The number one exercise to help you attain all of these benefits…is the one you will do! Warren, 151.

Back then we called it play, and we loved every minute of it. Today, for many, we call it exercise and count every minute of it, longing for it to be over. Warren, 161.

Exercise is good for the brain. It is helpful to include exercise that challenges the body and the mind a couple of times a week. Any sporting activity that makes you think will work. Join a team sport that requires you to move.

WELL*ACTS*

Are you too tired to serve God effectively? Confess your fatigue and ask the Lord to help you use your time wisely so that you can exercise and rest.

Are you willing to curtail your "rights" and "deny yourself" lawful pleasure to be at your best to serve the King? That may involve getting up a little earlier to exercise.

If you had sufficient energy and stamina, what would be your ministry goals?

Start with a few minutes of stretching exercises every morning. You can combine this with meditation by memorizing and reviewing Scripture passages as you stretch. See our website for suggestions.

Set a goal to walk at least 30 minutes each day. In the beginning, you may need to do a few short walks of ten minutes each until you build up your stamina. As you become fit, you may want to pick up the pace or expand the time of your walk. Walking also provides a good time for memorization and meditation. Exercise 30 minutes 5 times a week.

Take an unsaved or unchurched friend with you as you walk. Combine exercise and service.

When possible, walk instead of riding. Choose the stairs rather than the elevator.

Rest, Renew And Revitalize:
The Sabbath Rhythm

CHAPTER 8

Focal Texts: Genesis 2:2–3; Exod. 20:8–11; Luke 6:1–5

A study by the U.S. National Commission on Sleep Disorders blames half of all traffic accidents today on tiredness.[4] We are a nation running on empty! We are overscheduled, overweight, and overstressed. And we are feeling the whiplash effects in the workplace, the home, the church, even in our physical bodies. Fatigue is truly a killer.

Yet instead of running to get away from it—as people trying to remain survivors—we seem compelled to embrace it. Though we may complain to others about the pressure we're under, we somehow don't seem to know what we'd do without it. To hear most people talk about their life, they sound as if they're bragging about how much they're obligated to do and how little time it leaves them to rest and renew physically, emotionally, or spiritually.

So while all of us are in need of Sabbath, have we actually become somewhat allergic to it, perhaps even resistant to it? Do its legalistic prohibitions in Old Testament Scripture cause us not to want the limitations that a "day of rest" appears to entail? And even if we knew that the characteristics of Sabbath in the New Covenant look quite a bit different, are we still inclined to throw out the proverbial baby with the bath water? Are we neglecting a vital principle about the rhythm

---

[4] Carl Honore, *In Praise of Slowness (Plus)*, Location 137.

of life that we must rediscover if we are going to be *Well2Serve*?

The Sabbath Rhythm Established (Gen. 2:2–3)

The first mention of a "Sabbath rest" is found in the creation narrative. On the sixth day, God created man, male and female, blessed them, and gave them both the privilege and responsibility to rule over the earth (1:26–30). In other words, He gave them work to do. And God declared that all He had created—including work—was "very good," meaning it fully satisfied His purpose.

But "by the seventh day God completed His work which He had done, and He rested on the seventh day from all His work which He had done" (2:2). The fact that even God's creative activity is repeatedly called "work" is yet another way that He ascribes to human labor the highest possible dignity—because our work is modeled after God's work.

Therefore, God's decision to take a Sabbath rest at the conclusion of His creative activity was not an aversion to work, but rather the celebration of a completed task. Nor did God rest because He was fatigued. The omnipotent God is never exhausted; He never needs to "slumber or sleep" (Ps. 121:4). Further, His cessation from work was not permanent. He did not stop all activity from that point on. He ceased His creative work, but He continued (and continues) to work in other ways. He is not the legendary watchmaker of Deism who created the universe like a cosmic timepiece, wound it up, and then just let it tick away, unmonitored. God keeps up His redemptive labor on behalf of mankind even to this day.

Yet the word "rest" (sabat) is used twice in these two verses in reference to God, and thus we must consider its significance.

The Bible says that God "blessed" and "sanctified" the "seventh day" (2:3). In the same way that He "blessed" the man and woman, giving them both the capacity to multiply and the responsibility to manage the earth (1:28), He also blessed the Sabbath, meaning that both work and rest originate in Him and are pleasing to Him. The term "sanctified" means that the seventh day was set apart for God, "because in it He rested from all His work which God had created and made" (2:3). The fact that He sanctified it means He was establishing Sabbath rest as a principle for all of mankind, not just Himself, long before it would become more officially codified through the law.

One other observation: Day seven of creation does not end with the standard refrain from the first six days—"There was evening and there was morning." This is a deliberate omission which indicates that the rhythm of Sabbath has an infinite nature—that it continues today and will be enjoyed throughout eternity. Thus, every day is sacred in a sense (see Heb. 4:3–11; Col. 2:16–17), and should include some set-aside times for worship, rest, renewal, and reflection on the accomplishments of our labor, just as God paused on the original Sabbath to reflect on the glory of His own.

The Sabbath Rhythm Declared (Exod. 20:8–11; Deut. 2–15)

The command to "remember the Sabbath day, to keep it holy" is the fourth commandment—not a suggestion; a commandment. It forms a bridge between the first three (which focus on one's relationship to God) and the final six (which regulate one's relationship with his fellowman).

This specific command actually appears twice in Scripture, with slightly different emphases each time. In the Exodus account, the commandment concerning a Sabbath rest is specifically related to God's great work of creation. But when the law is restated in Deuteronomy 5:12–15, the focus is on Israel's redemption from bondage. "You shall remember that you were a slave in the land of Egypt, and the Lord your God brought you out of there by a mighty hand and by an outstretched arm; therefore the Lord your God commanded you to observe the sabbath day" (v. 15). So Sabbath is a celebration of God's activity in two arenas: in creation and redemption. Israel as a nation and its people individually belonged to God in two ways: they were created by Him and redeemed for Him.

As you read both passages—from Exodus 20 and Deuteronomy 5— notice that the Sabbath principle is comprehensive in nature. It was to include family members, servants, animals, even sojourners who may be visiting. And while many of the Ten Commandments are stated in a negative or prohibitive fashion— "thou shalt not"—this particular commandment is stated in a positive form: "Remember the sabbath day." Its life principle is for our delight and our good.

Yet we seem to misconstrue God's positive tone as almost a passive excuse for treating it casually. Few evangelical believers would ever boast about regularly violating any of the other commandments. Can you imagine someone declaring with a note of hardworking zeal that they routinely steal products from a store or that they lie repeatedly? Yet we don't mind bragging about how busy we are and how little time we have. We feel entitled to our activity because we think it defines us. Thus we not only violate the Sabbath rhythm of life, but we proudly do so—because we think our busyness gives us an air of importance.

The Sabbath Was Made for Man (Mark 2:23–28)

As we move this teaching into the New Testament, we come across an event which three of the Synoptic Gospels record: Jesus' disciples picking grain on the Sabbath (cf. Matt. 12:1–8; Luke 6:1–5). This occurrence led to the accusation that Jesus allowed His disciples to flippantly violate the Sabbath command of Scripture. But this charge was wholly unfounded. Jesus was merely introducing a higher way of approaching the law, and didn't mind pointing out the arrogance and hypocrisy in how some people tried to apply God's commands to their lives—or more specifically, how they applied it to others' lives.

If one's spirituality is determined by obedience to a set of rules, then it is necessary to make sure that one can clearly define those rules. And so for a legalist to argue that a person must cease from labor on the Sabbath, he must control what the word "labor" means and adjust it to his purposes. By the time of Jesus, the Pharisees had turned Sabbath enforcement into a cottage industry, developing 39 classifications of work to be avoided. As a result, they had turned it into a burden rather than a blessing—the very opposite of what its Lawgiver intended.

While these accounts from the various gospels differ in minor details, they all affirm two basic truths. First, the Sabbath was created for man. Mark states this principle in no uncertain terms—"The Sabbath was made for man, and not man for the Sabbath" (2:27). All three descriptions illustrate this truth by recounting the story of David and his companions who entered the house of God and ate the consecrated bread (see 1 Samuel 21:1–6). Matthew further references the particular law which allowed priests in the temple to work on the Sabbath and still remain innocent (Matt. 12:5)—sort of like pastors and church staff who carry out a significant portion of their jobs on Sunday. Jesus used these examples to show that the Sabbath was established for man's enjoyment and refreshment, not to appease the arcane control needs of the legalists. So the plucking of grain for an afternoon snack in no way violated the Sabbath principle, any more than Jesus' Sabbath day healing of a man with the withered hand. Since the Sabbath was created for man's benefit, it is to be a healing event in the full sense of the word.

Second, Jesus declared His lordship and authority over the Sabbath. The law of the Sabbath has now been brought to full fruition through Him. Thus it was perfectly acceptable for Jesus to reinterpret this law with God's original intention in mind. God created the Sabbath because He knew of man's need to rest and to be renewed in his entire being. But where laws and restrictions failed to empower man to fully embrace the Sabbath principle, Christ makes it possible for us to truly enter into its rest. So by affirming Himself as Lord of the Sabbath, He moves it into full alignment with His kingdom purposes. No longer should anyone treat it as an out-of-date Old Testament pronouncement. It is part of our response to His work in us today, and it will be part of our kingdom participation with Him for all eternity.

This is what makes Matthew's reporting of this scene so particularly refreshing. The passage that immediately precedes it is Jesus' well-known appeal for His people to find their rest in Him alone: "Come to Me, all who are weary and heavy laden, and I will give you rest. Take My yoke upon you and learn from Me, for I am gentle and humble in heart, and you will find rest for your souls. For My yoke is easy and My burden is light" (Matt. 11:28–30). This is truly what Sabbath rest is meant to provide us—not just on Sunday, but at all times. And ultimately for all time.

The Believer's Rest (Heb. 4:1–11)

The writer of Hebrews speaks of a Sabbath rest that remains for the people of God—a type of rest the people of Israel forfeited by not taking hold of the Promised Land under Moses' leadership. They failed because they didn't apply faith to what they heard from God (Heb. 4:2). But the reason why we know this rest is still in force is based on God's personal example of Sabbath rest (v. 4), which allowed Him to transition from His creative work to fully embrace His redemptive work, which was planned and completed before the "foundation of the world" (v. 3). That's how we grasp the significance of this passage.

If Israel had obediently entered into Canaan at the

early stages of her release from bondage, she could have ceased the work of possession in order to carry out her new work of world mission, to be lived out as a priestly people. Look at a map of the ancient world, and you'll see the highways of the nations running straight through Palestine. What better location for the reaching of all tribes and tongues.

But Israel was forced through disobedience to delay her greater activity because she had not yet accomplished her first work. And the writer to the Hebrews feared that his readers, too, might risk failing to enter the promised rest of God on similar grounds. Like Israel, they had accepted God's plan of redemption for themselves, but they were failing (perhaps because of persecution) to proclaim this plan of redemption to the world.

"So there remains a Sabbath rest for the people of God," the writer said (v. 9). He uses a word for rest (sabbatismos) which only occurs here in the New Testament and may actually have been coined by its author. Perhaps we should translate it as "a Sabbath kind of rest"—rest from dedication and preparation, in order to fulfill our work as kingdom agents. In other words, it is a Sabbath rest which enables us to serve God fully and effectively.[5]

What Are the Implications?

What conclusions can we draw from this study of Sabbath rest?

First, it establishes the nobility of our work and our need to delight in our labor. Second, it establishes

[5] Much of the understanding of this passage is based on Herschel H. Hobbs, *How to Follow Jesus* (Nashville, Broadman Press, 1971), pp. 41-46.

man's need to cease from, reflect upon, and enjoy his or her work. Third, it serves to restore one's vitality for continuing service. And fourth, it establishes a Sabbath rhythm to our life—not just weekly, but daily. It's part of being *Well2Serve*.

The pattern of work followed by rest, renewal, and revitalization was established for man's good and God's glory. It is more than a particular day or a 24-hour period where we perform a few religious duties; it is an overall rhythm of life.[6] At the end of each day, in fact, we should celebrate what God has caused us to accomplish, anticipating a night of rest as we allow Him to renew us in body, soul, and spirit, enabling us to serve Him effectively. Then at the end of each week, we need to set aside a day for celebration, worship, enjoyment, reflection, and rest as we prepare for the week ahead.

For Memory and Meditation

"Come to Me, all who are weary and heavy-laden, and I will give you rest" (Matt. 11:28).

---

[6] Dan B. Allender, *Sabbath*. Nashville: Thomas Nelson, 2009, p. 5. I recommend this thorough treatment on the Sabbath.

WELL*FACTS*

Relaxing is as important as breathing, sleeping, or eating. Not doing it will kill you. Hyman, 138.

But the truth is that most of us don't get enough sleep, and that plays a significant role in our aging. In fact, people who sleep fewer than six hours a night have a 50 percent increased risk of viral infections and an increased risk of heart disease and stroke. Roizen, 181.

Meditation seems to cause the release of melatonin to soothe your body and protect your own tissue-friendly stem cells. Roizen, 185.

When we feel disillusioned, depressed, gloomy, melancholy, lonely, and despairing, God's answer is to rest, eat, and drink. We cannot try to move forward with the normal daily routine without taking time to assess where we are. Hayles, 88.

Research has shown that people think more creatively when they are calm, unhurried, and free from stress, and that time pressure leads to tunnel vision. Honore, 121.

All the things that bind us together and make life worth living—community, family, friendship—thrive on the one thing we never have enough of: time. Honore, 11.

WELL*ACTS*

Do you find that you are sometimes "proud" of being so overworked that you don't take time to relax and reflect? Confess it as sin, and seek forgiveness and strength to find a Sabbath rhythm for life.

Develop a productive Sabbath rhythm which includes adequate sleep each night and a day for rest, reflection, and worship. Sleep seven to eight hours a night.

Suggestions to help with your nightly rest—get exercise daily; keep your bedroom cool and dark; no laptops or televisions in the bedroom; use white noise to block out outside noise; establish a routine related to going to bed and getting up; purchase the best mattress you can afford; read Scripture, pray, and meditate on God's Word each evening.

Take one day where you rest, reflect on your work, enjoy creativity, and worship God. We have already established the importance of community for your physical well-being; it is also an important aspect of worship. The writer to the Hebrews warns against forsaking the assembling together for mutual encouragement and worship (10:19–25). Find a church where worship is sincere and stimulating and the Bible is believed and taught.

Take a long walk and enjoy God's creation. Listen to your favorite music without interruption. Enjoy a museum or an arboretum. Spend quality time with your family and friends.

A Healthy Mind

CHAPTER 9

Focal Texts: Mark 1:28–30; Daniel 1:8;
Romans 7:23–25; 12:1–2; Philippians 4:8–9

Discoveries are regularly being made which suggest that the human mind is capable of more than we can imagine. Some experts believe it can store five times as much information as a complete set of the Encyclopedia Britannica—equivalent to 1000 terabytes worth of computer storage. (One terabyte alone, if you're counting, is equal to a trillion bytes.)

But more than its amazing capacity for memory, calculation, and other technical functions, the brain—serving as the command center of the body's entire nervous system—influences every square inch of us. In one sense, we truly are what we think! Our thoughts have the power to determine our mood, impact our behavior, and even affect our physical health. So when our thinking is transformed—as Romans 12:2 urges us—our entire view on ourselves and the world can be altered.

God is the one who created this marvel, and He has a lot to say about it in His Word. We would all be wise to seek it out . . . and to listen.

Love God with All Your Mind (Mark 12:28–31)

You may recall that we began this study by focusing on man's uniqueness, how we stand alone among all creatures by being fashioned in God's image. One aspect of man's uniqueness is his rational ability, which allows him to think, reason, and emote. It therefore is not surprising that when Jesus said the greatest commandment is to "love the Lord your God," He included our mind as one of the avenues through which we love Him. And because so much of everything else that takes place within our bodies is controlled by the mind, we see its interconnectedness as a way for God's truth and love to pervade us entirely. When we love God with our mind by studying, memorizing, and meditating on His Word (see Ps. 119:9–16), our whole being is blessed.

David's advice to Solomon reflects this holistic view of man. "As for you, my son Solomon, know the God of your father, and serve Him with a whole heart and a willing mind; for the Lord searches all hearts, and understands every intent of the thoughts" (1 Chron. 28:9a). David himself prayed, "Examine me, O Lord, and try me; test my mind and my heart" (Ps. 26:2).

Through the prophet Jeremiah, God declares, "I, the Lord, search the heart, I test the mind, even to give to each man according to his ways, according to the results of his deeds" (Jer. 17:10 and cf. 20:12). If God desires that we love Him with our minds, we should not be surprised that He tests our minds, to see where our thoughts are dwelling.

Several years ago, apologist Os Guiness wrote a book entitled *Fit Bodies, Fat Minds*. The subtitle tells the story—"Why Evangelicals Don't Think and What to Do about It."[7] Are we guilty of desiring faith without thought? Have we ignored the command to love God with our mind?

---

[7] Os Guinness, *Fit Bodies Fat Minds* (Baker Books; Grand Rapids, Michigan), 1994.

The Mind Is the Seat of Conviction (Dan. 1:8)

We've looked already at the story of Daniel and his friends who were conscripted into service by Babylon's pagan king Nebuchadnezzar. But our earlier focus was more on the healthy diet that Daniel chose for himself, as opposed to the heavy foods and wine which his captors tried to force on him. What I want you to see now is this: Daniel "made up his mind" that he would not defile himself by what he allowed into his body (v. 8). His conviction led him to make a clear decision that radically impacted his behavior. You and I will make little progress in applying the principles shared in our study together until we, like Daniel, are willing to make up our minds to do it.

In the book of Romans, Paul deals with an issue concerning the appropriate day for worship. "One person regards one day above another, another regards every day alike." Paul's advice? "Each person must be fully convinced in his own mind" (Rom. 14:5). Conviction is centered in the mind, which leads us to adopt actions that match.

Here is a wonderful promise that will challenge you to live by settled conviction: "The steadfast of mind You will keep in perfect peace, because he trusts in You" (Isa. 26:3). As you are studying each chapter of this book, ask God to give you clarity of mind concerning His desire and design for you. Once you hear His voice, write down your decision and allow the Holy Spirit to empower you to stand upon your conviction.

The Mind Is a Spiritual Battleground (Rom. 7:23–25)

Romans 7 is a passage with which many of us can readily identify, especially in keeping ourselves *Well2Serve*. Paul confesses his aggravating tendency to do the things he hates to do (v. 15). He concludes, after several verses of frustrating logic, that the flesh is weak and always susceptible to such struggles. "For the good that I want, I do not do, but I practice the very evil that I do not want" (v. 19). Does this sound like the dilemma you face as you try to make changes that lead to total wellness?

Paul finally cries out, begging for freedom from the law of sin which is in his body (v. 23)—but not before voicing a note of victory: "Thanks be to God through Jesus Christ our Lord!" (v. 25)—for even with our constant struggles, there is no condemnation for those in Christ Jesus (8:1). Because of the new birth, Paul sees a new law at work in himself which enables him to overcome the power of sin working in the members of his body—"the law of the Spirit of life in Christ Jesus" (v. 2).

Again, each of us understands the battle that takes place between our ears. Whether you're having trouble controlling your eating, getting enough rest and exercise, thinking on God's Word, lowering your stress, dumping your toxic attitudes, or overriding your natural sense of laziness and apathy, remember—you have the Spirit of life within you through the power of Christ Jesus!

Notice the role of the mind as it relates to spiritual victory: "For those who are according to the flesh set their minds on the things of the flesh, but those who are according to the Spirit, the things of the Spirit. For the mind set on the flesh is death, but the mind set on the Spirit is life and peace" (8:5-6). If you want life and peace, focusing your mind on Him is critical.

We see several examples in the Bible, both good and bad, that show how our thinking clearly impacts behavior. Nehemiah speaks of the motivation that prompted the Israelites to rebuild the wall, "for the people had a mind to work" (Neh. 4:6). When his motives were questioned by his detractors, he said they were inventing these accusations in their own minds (6:8). Their thought processes were what led them toward inaccurate conclusions, causing them to stand against Nehemiah's leadership.

The Bible speaks of a "depraved mind" on a number of occasions (1 Tim. 6:5; 2 Tim. 3:8–9). Paul talks about how the state of the Colossian Christians before their conversion was one of alienation and hostility of mind, which led them to evil deeds (Col. 1:21). One of the most tragic outcomes of a depraved mind is that God ultimately will give us over to the consequences caused by our own choices. If we continue to keep our minds corrupted with unrighteousness, wickedness, greed, evil, envy, murder, strife, deceit, and malice (Rom. 1:28–32), we will become mired so deeply in deception that we cannot find the way out. (We will look further at these toxic attitudes in chapter 11.)

But be encouraged as you seek to love God with the entirety of your thoughts, because the Spirit of life in Christ Jesus dwells in you. And He will continually fight for you in the battle for your mind.

The Renewing of the Mind (Rom. 12:1–2)

The problem we face, even as believers, is that we can still be controlled by old patterns of thinking that are part of our upbringing and culture. These thoughts are like tapes that seem to turn themselves on at the worst possible moment, discouraging us from believing that we can change. They may come from our past, those times when someone told us we would never amount to much, or that we would always be overweight . . . the list could go on and on.

So how do we make the transition from thoughts that discourage us and keep us from living with purpose and meaning, turning them into thoughts that bring life and peace? What we need is transformation, and the Bible tells us how this occurs.

1. Transformation requires a volitional choice. Paul tells the Roman believers to present themselves to God. God will strengthen and empower you, but you must choose to present yourself totally to Him. Perhaps you should stop right now and pray something like this: "Lord, I give You my mind. I choose to think Your thoughts and not those of the world." Amen!

2. Refuse to be conformed to the world. The "world" in this context stands for the world order that sets itself against the things of God—a world that is already passing away and is dominated by "the god of this world," who desires to blind the eyes of the unbelieving (2 Cor. 4:4). Only by the power of God's Spirit can we resist the tendency to live by the standards of this age. Don't let the shortsighted values of the world lead you to conformity and mediocrity.

3. Be continually transformed by the renewing of

your mind. You have a choice: you will either be conformed or be transformed. There is no neutral ground here. The word translated "transformed" is the Greek metamorphoo, the same word which comes across as "transfigure" in the transfiguration passages from Matthew and Mark. The only other occurrence of this term in the New Testament is 2 Corinthians 3:18, where Paul speaks of believers being changed into the likeness of Christ by degrees. Perhaps you heard the English word "metamorphosis" as you attempted to read the Greek word metamorphoo. It's true—you can experience a butterfly-like transformation as you break free from the cocoon of thinking that has trapped you in unhealthy and unproductive patterns of living. Replace old ways of thinking with new productive ways that are based on biblical truth—reading, memorizing, meditating upon, and obeying God's truth in every area of your life.

Discoveries from medical science concerning issues such as eating, exercising, resting, etc., regularly confirm the truths that God has already given us from the beginning. It shouldn't surprise us that the Creator who loved us enough to send His Son to redeem us would also give us principles which would, when obeyed, lead to total fitness.

4. Transformation entails productive service. Paul declares that the end goal of transformation is that "you may prove what the will of God is" (Rom. 12:2)—that you will know it and do it. The impact of sin and our own susceptibility to it have led us away from that which man was created for. But we can even now be changed—continually, daily, over and over again—by

the correcting influence of God's Spirit on our minds. We can be transformed to serve Him effectively, head to toe.

The Proper Focus of the Transformed Mind (Phil. 4:8–9)

Paul's concluding thought on how to life a joyful and peaceful life concerns the proper focus of one's mind. "Finally, brethren, whatever is true, whatever is honorable, whatever is right, whatever is pure, whatever is lovely, whatever is of good repute, if there is any excellence and if anything worthy of praise, dwell on these things" (Phil. 4:8).

The word translated "dwell" means much more than casual thought. It means "to reckon," "to take into account," "to use one's mental facilities on." We might use a word like "meditation" today to translate this word. In addition, the verb carries an imperative meaning. It is not a suggestion, but a command. And it is in the present tense, meaning we should do it as a continual practice. Dwelling on the purity and beauty of God's truth must become the default button for all our thought processes.

We should be meditating on it—all the time.

Sadly, many evangelical believers see meditation as an invention of mystical religion, such as that practiced by many in the New Age movement. But the concept of meditation is a consistent teaching of God's Word. Consider Joshua 1:8—"This book of the law shall not depart from your mouth, but you shall meditate on it day and night, so that you may be careful to do according to all that is written in it; for then you will make your way prosperous, and then you will have success."

Meditation is a healthy practice if we follow biblical standards. We don't simply empty our minds by repeating some nonsensical mantra. No, we meditate on Scripture—on those things that are true, honorable, right, pure, lovely, of good repute, things that are excellent and worthy of praise.

And before we know it, our thoughts will lead to concrete action. Paul commands his readers in verse 9 to "practice" the things they have heard from and seen in him. Once again the verb is a present imperative, indicating it is a command requiring repetitive action. The issue of the mind is not a once and done; it is a daily and continuous action.

And the result? Whole lives that are driven by truth and power to keep our commitments and to serve Him mightily.

For Memory and Meditation

"The steadfast of mind You will keep in perfect peace, because he trusts in You" (Isa. 26:3).

But the truth is that even if your genes have decided to give you a life of serious forgetfulness, you do have the ability to control those genes so your mind is strong, your brain functions at full power, and you remember everything from the crucial details of your life to whether or not you turned off the oven—even when your birthday candles reach triple digits. Roizen, 27.

You don't need to have an elite brain to know that your three-pound organ has more power than a rocket booster. It controls everything from your emotions to your decision making. Roizen,30.

Like babies and brats, all your brain wants is this: attention. Feed it, challenge it, care for it, and you'll smack a bad genetic destiny square in the face with five knuckles of good information and smart action. One of the key things to do is constantly stretch your mind. Roizen, 41.

When you increase your learning during life, you decrease the risk of developing memory-related problems. That means your brain has a fighting chance if you keep it active and engaged, if you keep challenging it with new lessons. Roizen, 41.

WELL*ACTS*

Exercising the brain is one of the most important steps you can take to keep it operating at maximum efficiency. Memorize the twelve verses that are part of this study. Next, memorize entire chapters of the Bible. You will be stimulating both mind and spirit.

Teaching can save your brain. When you volunteer to teach, you are maximizing the effects of memory and service, thus getting a double benefit. You can volunteer to teach at a local school, a church, or a community organization.

Reading this book and discussing this material is a step in the right direction. Be a lifelong learner. Read consistently, even if you struggle with reading. The process will keep your brain healthy. Sign up for a course at a local school just for the fun of it.

Your diet impacts your brain. Among the best nutrients to help keep your cerebral power lines strong are omega-3 fatty acids—the kinds of fat found in fish like salmon and mahi-mahi. Aim for 13 ounces of fish a week, or, if you prefer supplements, take 2 grams of fish oil a day (metabolically distilled), or DHA from algae, or an ounce of walnuts a day (Roizen, 43).

Consider detoxifying your life by avoiding all chemical sweeteners.

Learn to tell a good joke. Laughter is good for the soul, and the mental acuity required to tell a joke is good for the brain.

CHAPTER 10

Handling Stress: The Silent Killer

Focal Text: Philippians 4:4–9

Clinical research is confirming what most all of us have known from personal experience: stress (along with the accompanying emotion of anxiety) is a killer.

A study which combined the results from 101 smaller studies, incorporating research on several thousand men and women, reveals that perturbing emotions are truly bad for our health. "People who experienced chronic anxiety, long periods of sadness and pessimism, unremitting tension or incessant hostility, relentless cynicism or suspiciousness, were found to have double the risk of disease—including asthma, arthritis, headaches, peptic ulcers, and heart disease (each representative of major, broad categories of disease). This order of magnitude makes distressing emotions as toxic a risk factor as, say, smoking or high cholesterol are for heart disease."[8]

Further, stress can have an adverse impact on our behavior. "Stress of all sorts creates adrenocortical arousal, lowering the threshold for what provokes anger. Thus someone who has had a hard day at work is especially vulnerable to becoming enraged later at home by something . . . that under other circumstances would not be powerful enough to trigger an emotional hijacking."[9]

So in thinking about our overall health and our

---

[8] Daniel Goleman, *Emotional Intelligence: 10th Anniversary Edition*, Kindle, location 3443.

[9] Ibid., location 1361.

desire to be completely available for God's use, it is worth our time to explore ways to cope with stress. By handling it well and responding to it biblically, we can resist the undertow of destructive anxiety by submerging it in joyous celebration and personal growth.

A famous study by Drs. Richard Lazarus and Susan Folkman revealed that the effects of stress could be tempered or amplified by our assessment of the situation and our ability to deal with it. "The effects of a stressful challenge are not simply a result of the challenge itself; they also greatly depend on our responses." These researchers discovered that people who handled stress well viewed it as a challenge, believed they could have some control over what happened to them, and were committed to make the best of it. Their response to stress protected them from the adverse physical reactions.[10]

Paul, then, was obviously ahead of his time in providing a strategy for positively coping with stress and anxiety. His advice will serve each of us well. Let's explore it together.

Rejoice in the Lord Always (v. 4)

When difficult circumstances interrupt the normal flow of life, Philippians 4 is one of those passages that not only gives perspective but gives us some practical tools for dealing with it. Structurally, the passage includes three imperative verbs followed by a promise—meaning, these are not just helpful suggestions. They are commands which, when followed, will lead

---

[10] Martin Rossman, *The Worry Solution: Using Breakthrough Brain Science to Turn Stress and Anxiety into Confidence and Happiness*, Kindle, location 501.

us toward peaceful hearts that defy our surroundings. From the look of things, we should be falling apart. But instead—beyond all comprehension—we are still standing strong. And still *Well2Serve*.

The phrase "rejoice in the Lord always" (Phil. 4:4) can only mean that joy is much different from happiness. Happiness is often related to one's circumstances and thus can vary according to external events. Things or people can make us respond with happiness or unhappiness. Joy, however, is like an underground stream, flowing unabated by conditions on the surface. Truly in every circumstance, we can still find joy "in the Lord" . . . always!

Paul knew this truth by both experience and revelation, which inspired him to write such verses as Romans 8:28: "And we know that God causes all things to work together for good to those who love God, to those who are called according to His purpose."

Notice first what Romans 8:28 does not say. It does not say that God causes "all things," including the evil in our lives; He just causes all things to "work together for good." God is holy, cannot be tempted by evil, and cannot tempt anyone else to evil (James 1:13). So when these difficult, stressful situations arise in our lives— whether through our own poor choices, another's poor choices, or perhaps merely as a result of living in a fallen world—the most important thing to remember is that God can still do something about it.

What we usually want Him to do is to take it away. That's how we'd like him to work everything "for good." God's "good," on the other hand, is to work in every circumstance to conform us to the image of His own

Son (Rom. 8:29), no matter how difficult the challenge may seem.

Later in Romans 8, Paul speaks of some of the ordeals faced by the first-century believers. His list is comprehensive, including life and death, things present and things yet to come, angels and principalities, height and depth, and every created thing. But the bottom line of such daily circumstances is that nothing can separate us from the love of God—or from His ability and desire to bring about ultimate good as a result.

This passage became even more precious to our Southwestern seminary family when a number of young people were killed and wounded in the mass shooting at Wedgwood Baptist Church in Fort Worth. Dr. Jack McGorman, addressing our chapel during the days following, used this text to declare that the omniscient God was not caught unaware, and the omnipotent God was able to bring good out of these evil circumstances.

For this reason, our first response to circumstances which have the potential to produce anxiety within us is to "rejoice" in our knowledge that God is bigger than every one of them. Every circumstance can be viewed as a challenge that enables us to experience more of God.

Exhibit a Gentle Spirit (v. 5)

Gentleness is often looked upon by the world as a sign of weakness, but Paul would declare it to be one of the characteristics of Christ that he attempted to model for others (2 Cor. 10:1). The word used here includes the idea of humble and patient steadfastness, which is able to submit to injustice, disgrace, and mis-treatment without hatred or malice.

Gentleness requires selflessness in the most positive sense. It keeps us from insisting on our rights or seeing difficulties as a personal affront, as if we don't deserve them. When we fully comprehend that what we all deserve is death because of our sin (Rom. 6:23), and yet have received forgiveness instead because of Christ's gift, we gain a whole different perspective on life's difficult circumstances.

The person who doesn't exhibit a gentle spirit will often rail at life as if he or she is the only one facing problems. When injured by another, such a person may attempt to get even or punish the offender. But this is the kind of response that arises from man's foolish belief that we are wiser than God. You and I can resolve much of our anxiety if we simply relax and let God be God.

The basis of our gentle spirit is an awareness that "the Lord is near" (v. 5). We can take three truths from this simple statement. First, in every circumstance, no matter how challenging, we can still experience God's presence. The psalmist writes, "When my anxious thoughts multiply within me, Your consolations delight my soul" (Ps. 94:19). Second, it reminds us of His sure return, when He will establish Himself as righteous judge. "Say to those with anxious heart, 'Take courage, fear not. Behold, your God will come with vengeance; the recompense of God will come, but He will save you'" (Isa. 35:4). Finally, it assures us that when He returns, He will establish His righteous kingdom.

With all these certainties in mind, we can lead ourselves to experience gentleness in our spirit.

Ban Anxiety with Prayer and Thanksgiving (v. 6)

While the phrase "be anxious for nothing" is a negative imperative, it maintains a positive thrust. We must refuse to be fretful and anxious in regard to anything.

Immediately after teaching His disciples how to pray (Matt. 6:9–13), Jesus asks them a pointed question: "And who of you by being worried can add a single hour to his life?" (v. 27). Read the remainder of Matthew 6, and you will find the word "worry" repeated five times—three of which are in the form of an imperative. Jesus commands them not to worry— about any of the stuff of life: their food, their clothes, their death, their future. On what basis? Because "your heavenly Father knows that you need all these things" (v. 32). Thus we can replace worry by seeking God's kingdom and not our own. Worry produces only negative results, which has a profound effect on our health and attitude toward life. If only we could accept God's complete ban on worry—just imagine what this one change in conviction could do!

Now we can't ban anxiety simply by "trying harder," by telling ourselves not to worry. In truth, our striving to ban anxiety will only produce greater anxiety, making us focus more on the events that are causing our anxiety. Instead, we must replace anxiety by prayer and supplication accompanied by thanksgiving.

Notice the contrast created by "be anxious for nothing," and "in everything by prayer." Prayer is not a formal recitation of words reserved for specified times; it is the very breath of the Christian's existence.

The phrase "let your requests be made known to God" translates a present active imperative verb. Prayer is an ongoing habitual dialogue with our Father, who knows our needs and who desires to answer our requests according to His perfect plans for our lives. There is no concern too small to bring to God.

But that's not all. Our prayers and supplications (specific requests arising from a special need) should be addressed to God "with thanksgiving." Thanksgiving is the distinctive mark of the believer. It sets us in contrast with the nonbeliever who fails to give thanks (Rom. 1:21). Thanksgiving is the grateful acknowledgement of past blessings and the present confidence of God's desire to work in our every circumstance for good. We can affirm with Paul, "For if while we were enemies we were reconciled to God through the death of His Son, much more, having been reconciled, we shall be saved by His life" (Rom. 5:10). Simply put, the believer must face all adversity with an attitude of gratitude. Gratitude for God's saving grace! Gratitude for His constant care! Gratitude for the assurance of His promised redemption!

When you think about the issues that create the most anxiety, aren't they often circumstances that are beyond our personal control? In this context, Paul speaks to a time when the Philippians lacked the opportunity to provide financial support for his mission work. No doubt, this financial hardship could have caused Paul great anxiety. He chose to respond, however, by viewing it as an opportunity to see God at work. He testified that he had learned to be content in every circumstance: "I know how to get along with humble means, and I also know how to live in prosperity; in any and every circumstance I have learned the secret of being filled and going hungry, both of having abundance and suffering need. I can do all things through Him who strengthens me" (Phil. 4:12–13).

When I became president of Southwestern Seminary, we were placed on probation by one of our accrediting associations. Needless to say, this development was met with the expected "wringing of hands" and "gnashing of teeth" over the future of the institution. But I believed the Lord had given me a word to deliver to the seminary family, which has since become somewhat of a motto for our family. "Difficult circumstances provide the platform on which God displays His supernatural activity." Would you rather destroy your life with worry or see God at work?

The Peace of God, Guarding Our Hearts and Minds (v. 7)

Nothing about this passage gives us a promise that our external circumstances will always be altered or that our earthly needs will immediately be met. But in fact, the promise here is much greater than these temporal adjustments. We are promised that the "peace of God" will "guard" our hearts and minds.

The word "guard" is a military term which pictures soldiers standing on duty, posted inside of the gate, controlling all who desire to enter. The gate guarded by God's peace is the one that surrounds our hearts and minds. As we have already noted, the heart is the center of one's being from which our thoughts and affections flow. The mind controls the acts of will and thus impacts our behavior. And these two invaluable components of our makeup—our hearts and minds—are guarded by a peace which is divine in origin and character. For that reason, this peace "surpasses all comprehension."

As a pastor of many years, I have been privileged to experience in my own life and to witness in the lives of others this peace which "surpasses all comprehension." I remember visiting a young lady from Southwestern who had moved to a dangerous mission field soon after marriage. In an unprovoked attack, her husband was killed and she herself was severely wounded. As Paula and I stood by her hospital bed and inquired how we could pray for her, she simply requested that we pray for her attackers and the people of that region of the world who were lost without Christ. She could easily have been embittered by her circumstances, yet she chose God's peace . . . which surpasses comprehension.

You don't have to understand all of life's circumstances. And you will not always see how God can work "good" in the "everything" of your life. But you can be assured that His peace will put a guard on your heart and mind. And when He does—through your rejoicing, your gentleness, your refusal to fret and worry—a lot of what you now know as stress will not even be able to get a foot inside the door.

For Memory and Meditation
"Be anxious for nothing, but in everything by prayer and supplication with thanksgiving let your requests be made known to God" (Phil. 4:6).

WELL*FACTS*

A significant number of physical complaints and serious diseases have been linked to anxiety, including cardiovascular disease, ulcers, irritable bowel syndrome, and illnesses related to decreased immune function. Colbert, 110.

In many of these people, worry simply becomes a mental habit. They automatically tend to see events in their lives in terms of worst-case scenarios. As with any mental habit that becomes ingrained in the brain, this habit of general worry tends to get worse over time. Colbert, 108f.

A Harvard Medical School study of 1,623 heart attack survivors concluded that anger brought on by emotional conflicts doubled the risk of subsequent heart attacks compared to those who remain calm. Colbert, 9.

Anxiety—the distress evoked by life's pressures—is perhaps the emotion with the greatest weight of scientific evidence connecting it to the onset of sickness and course of recovery. Goleman, Kindle 3525.

It is your perception of something that turns it into a stressor (threat) to your well-being. As soon as a stressor exists in your mind, you have stress. Leman, location 375.

Feeling responsible for things over which you have no control is a sure way to put yourself under tremendous stress. Leman, location 1709.

WELL*ACTS*

What are the issues that cause you the most anxiety and stress? Which of them are issues you can change? Make the adjustments necessary to reduce anxiety and stress in those areas over which you possess control.

What are the issues that cause you anxiety and stress that you can't change? Commit these to the Lord in prayer with thanksgiving. Mark it in your journal when you surrender them.

Develop a regular habit of journaling your daily blessings.

When you are tempted to fall into the mental habit of worrying, choose to voice your praise instead. Negative patterns must be replaced with positive ones.

When you are feeling stress from anxiety, practice simple relaxation techniques such as deep diaphragm breathing and meditation. Meditation on the promises of God will help relieve stress.

Do something thoughtful for another person. Stress often results from our own myopia. To counteract it, we can focus on the needs of another. Do something positive for a team member.

Look for opportunities to smile regularly. Smile at the antics of children. Smile at friends, neighbors, employees, even enemies. A smile will lift their spirits as well as yours. Enjoy several good laughs each day.

Eliminating Toxic Emotions

Focal Text: Ephesians 4:17–32

You may not realize it, but when you work at managing your upset feelings—anger, anxiety, depression, pessimism, loneliness, and the like—you are actually engaging in a form of disease prevention. Yes, current data suggests that the toxicity of such emotions, when allowed to become chronic, is on a par with the dangers of smoking cigarettes. This means the medical payoff you derive from learning how to rid yourselves of them can be as great as what happens when heavy smokers kick their nicotine habit.[11]

So if you can steadily begin replacing anger, bitterness, and anxiety with joy, hope, forgiveness, and general optimism, you can potentially lengthen your life and—best of all—increase your effectiveness as a kingdom citizen.

Life Is a Series of Choices (vv. 17–24)

The mind, of course, is the center of cognition where we make important life decisions that ultimately influence our behavior, our total wellness, and our eternal impact. So as people ascribed by God with great value—people who can make enormous differences in the lives of others—we need to be making choices every day that continually affirm our created purpose.

That makes this section of Ephesians an important,

---

[11] Daniel Goleman, *Emotional Intelligence: 10th Anniversary Edition*, Kindle book, location 3757.

encouraging place of study, because it is all about making the kinds of choices that lead to a productive life. The term "walk" in verse 17 literally means "the daily conduct of one's life." Two options exist: people can walk "in the futility of their mind" (v. 17) or they can "be renewed in the spirit of [their] mind" (v. 23). "Futility of mind" is a perspective on life that totally disregards one's Creator and purpose. No matter how successful or prosperous one might appear to be, when persons live without regard for the Creator, they are missing the whole point of life.

No wonder the psalmist could declare that the person who says in his heart, "There is no God," is nothing short of a "fool" (Ps. 14:1a). When people ignore God and His directions concerning purposeful living, they allow themselves to be darkened in their understanding. Sure, such persons may still accumulate knowledge, but not true wisdom—because they're beginning from a false premise. And anytime we start in the wrong place, we are certain of reaching a disastrous destination. To choose spiritual ignorance is ultimately to choose hardness of heart and insensitivity to spiritual truth (Eph. 4:18).

Paul gives a simple three-step formula for effective Christian living which we must follow as we consider what it means to be *Well2Serve*.

1. "Put off" or "lay aside" the old self (v. 22). This means to completely abandon all the thinking processes and behavior patterns that belong to the old way of life. The Greek tense of the verb used here indicates a decisive act, a volitional turning from an "old," futile way of life. It's deliberate, active, and on purpose. And

it's more than just the one-time act of salvation. While conversion to Christ is certainly necessary before the "old self" can be effectively abandoned, its practical death is the product of many ongoing daily decisions.

No doubt our study has revealed some "old" behavior patterns which have impacted your wellness and your service. You may not have considered very often the significant impact such matters as diet, exercise, rest, and controlling your emotions can make on your spiritual life. But before you can establish the new kinds of patterns that put you in prime position to be of maximum usefulness to God, you must choose to put off some of your old ways of doing things. But don't worry—no matter how resistant or powerless you've felt in these areas before, God's Spirit provides you the strength to make decisions that can extend your life and increase the quality of your life.

2. "Be renewed in the spirit of your mind" (v. 23). Again, this is a present tense verb which indicates the need for continual renewal. Just as we must decisively and consistently "put off" the old way of thinking and behaving, we must continually be renewed in our thinking. We have already looked at this principle in great detail, particularly in chapter 9, but again, the Scripture is clear and consistent throughout. Mental renewal is foundational to starting fresh and staying sharp, both spiritually and physically.

3. "Put on the new self, which in the likeness of God has been created in righteousness and holiness of the truth" (v. 24). In Colossians, Paul describes the Christian as one who has "put on the new self which is being renewed to a true knowledge according to the im-

age of the One who created him" (Col. 3:10). The Holy Spirit indwells us so that we may be progressively and comprehensively renewed. In 2 Corinthians 3:18, Paul speaks of the work of the Spirit who enables us to be transformed from glory to glory into God's image. Each day and each choice builds on another. Our choices either take us forward, or they sink us back into apathy and futility.

I want you to be encouraged about the choices God has prompted you to make so that you can be *Well2Serve*. Every life-style change involves difficult daily choices, but you are not confined to willpower alone. The Holy Spirit has been given to empower you to make choices that will lead to a healthy and productive life. Further, you will have other believers standing beside you and encouraging you to choose total wellness. Our need for community cannot be overstated.

Five Healthy Life-style Choices (vv. 25–32)

You have probably heard the old adage, "When you see a 'therefore' in Scripture, see what it is 'there for.'" The "therefore" in verse 25 indicates that Paul is now making practical applications from the truths of the transformed life-style. He is taking this "old self/new self" discussion out of the realm of spiritual theory and laying it right down on the running track of real life. Again, this is because salvation transforms the totality of our entire person. Not only does Christ's gift of Himself change us spiritually and motivate us physically, but it is also meant to renew us emotionally.

Paul looks at five specific areas in this passage. Notice that a negative behavior must be replaced by a corresponding positive one, or your wellness choices will be short-lived.

1. Choose to live in community with integrity (v. 25). Does it surprise you that Paul's first application of the "new man" principle is related to the believer's life in community? While salvation is and must be an individual decision, it will always have a corporate dynamic to it. And in our dealings with one another, we must always be sure that we are not operating in dishonesty. "Falsehood" is characteristic of the old man and must be discarded—replaced with truth. The phrase "speak truth each one of you with His neighbor" is a quotation from Zechariah 8:16, yet with an important modification. The "to" in Zechariah is changed to "with" in Ephesians, emphasizing the integral connection of one member to another in the body of Christ. Since truth is in Jesus (v. 21), those who are alive in Him should manifest integrity in all their speech, even when needing to speak hard truth in love (v. 15). Honest speech promotes growth in all areas of our Christian life.

2. Choose to deal constructively with your anger (vv. 26–27). Paul moves next to anger, which can also negatively impact our relationship with fellow members. The saying, "Be angry, and yet do not sin," is from Psalm 4:4. Note that anger itself is not a sin; anger is a natural human emotion. Jesus, for instance, exhibited righteous anger against the pollution of the temple. (One note of warning here: What we call "righteous indignation," is often little more than our wounded pride.) But if we are serious about dealing effectively with our anger, one of the best methods for keeping it in check is to limit its duration: "Do not let the sun go

down on your anger" (v. 26).

Personally, when I submit my anger to the Lord, I attempt to resolve the issue causing the anger that very day. When it is beyond my ability to do so, I at least attempt to reconcile it in my heart by forgiving the person causing the offense and choosing not to become bitter. Such a response to anger is critical not only to my spiritual well-being but also to that of the church. If I nurse hurt feelings and become bitter, the Bible says that I provide the devil an opportunity to exploit my anger for his purposes.

Research has shown that anger has a devastating physical impact on your body. Dr. Don Colbert indicates that emotions such as anger produce a chemical reaction that impacts us at both the organ level and the cellular level. A Harvard Medical School study of 1,623 heart attack survivors concluded that anger brought on by emotional conflicts doubled the risk of subsequent heart attacks compared to those who remained calm. If the brain interprets physical perceptions as anger, fear, or depression, every immune cell of the body is aware of it very quickly.[12]

See why it is so critical that we resolve our anger issues quickly? If you are going to be *Well2Serve*, anger must be shown the door in a quick, deliberate, good riddance manner.

3. Choose to be a giver, not a taker (v. 28). Some of the early believers were thieves prior to their conversion. And not only did they need to give up stealing, they needed to replace this negative life-style with one

---

[12] Don Colbert, *Deadly Emotions* (Nashville: Thomas Nelson, 2003), pp. 9-13.

of meaningful labor, so that instead of taking from others, they would be supplied with excess to share with those in need. The Christian welcomes hard work as the duty of every authentic believer (cf. 1 Thess. 4:11; 2 Thess. 3:1–12). To the Christian, giving provides the proper motivation for getting.

People typically fall into one of two categories: givers or takers. And those who choose to be "givers" experience benefits in the present age as well as in the one to come. Throughout this study, we have noticed that our motivation for seeking whole life wellness is aimed at enabling us to become more effective servants. Healthy people are people who seek to enrich the lives of others. It's a choice that keeps us much happier—and much less toxic.

4. Choose to replace unwholesome speech with words that edify (vv. 29–30). The term "unwholesome" has the connotation of "rotten" or "worthless." The tongue can be a powerful weapon for evil or a tool for good. The believer is charged with replacing foul, worthless language with words that are timely and constructive, giving grace to those who hear. King Solomon wrote, "A man has joy in an apt answer, and how delightful is a timely word!" (Prov. 15:23). In Colossians 4:6, Paul speaks of speech which, like salt, adds flavor to the life of the hearer. My dad taught me to ask myself three questions before I speak: "Is it true? Is it necessary? Is it edifying?" Ask yourself—"Do my words hurt or heal?"

Paul's earlier instructions about dealing with anger were followed with the warning about giving the devil an opportunity. This instruction about our speech is also followed by a warning: not to grieve the Holy Spirit (v. 30). In fact, this warning is given gravity by the full reference: "the Holy Spirit of God." Sins of the tongue are felt by the Holy Spirit who indwells both the speaker and the listener. We have been sealed in Christ by the Spirit (Eph. 1:13), thus our speech must reflect His presence in our lives.

5. Choose to replace bitterness with forgiveness (v. 31). Bitterness is a poisonous attitude that develops when we refuse reconciliation. "Wrath" in this verse can also be translated "rage"— the result of unresolved anger. Paul often lists wrath and anger together (cf. Rom. 2:8; Col. 3:8) because they speak of the quick, often uncontrolled outbursts of anger caused by personal provocation. "Clamor" describes the angry person who desires that everyone hear his or her grievance, with hopes of receiving their pity. "Slander" translates the Greek word which means "blasphemy," a word often used of one who speaks against God. See the connection? When we slander our fellow believer—who bears the image of Christ—we blaspheme God. "Malice" involves bad feelings of every kind.

So Paul just declares war on all of it—total abstinence from every thought and emotion that would lead us to speak against or do evil to another.

Once again, Paul ends by inspiring us toward the positive behavior patterns which must replace the destructive ones (v. 32). "Kindness" is love made practical. The world considers the tenderhearted person an easy mark, a pushover. But the Bible views him as strong, steady, and Christlike, readily offering forgiveness because he operates from the perspective of one who has been forgiven. We must forgive freely and completely, even when it appears that forgiveness is underserved. After all, isn't that how God forgave us?

But remember—whether we're dealing with our anger, our harshness, our bitterness, or our greedy ingratitude—we are not just working through Sunday school material. We are leading out with a transformed mind toward a full body experience of health and wholeness. To stamp out these toxic emotions is to enliven our entire being with new joy and energy for Christ.

For Memory and Meditation

"Put on the new self, which in the likeness of God has been created in righteousness and holiness of the truth" (Eph. 4:24).

WELL*FACTS*

Generous acts strengthen the bonds of friendship and what's more, studies show that your happiness is often boosted more by providing support to other people than from receiving support yourself. Rubin, Kindle 2438.

Certain emotions release hormones into the physical body that, in turn, can trigger the development of a host of diseases. Colbert, xi.

Without a doubt, hostility, rage, and anger are at the top of the list of toxic emotions that generate an extreme stress reaction. Colbert, 35.

Ichiro Kawachi, of the Harvard School of Public Health, also has reported studies that link anger and coronary heart disease. He has written, "The relative risk of heart attack among angry patients looks as strong as it is from hypertension or smoking. Clinicians should screen their patients for a history of anger, and consider referring them to counseling or anger management therapy." Colbert, 40.

The good news is that you can do a great deal to pull the plug on these toxic emotions that fuel deadly and painful diseases. You can do much to improve your physical health by addressing first and foremost your emotional health. Colbert, xii.

WELL*ACTS*

Deal constructively with anger:

1) When you sense yourself becoming angry, take 10 deep breaths as you thank God for the gift of life. The attitude of gratitude is the best cure for anger.

2) Deal with anger immediately. Refuse to let the sun go down on your anger.

3) Apologize to others for your angry response. Don't get hung up with the questions of who started it or who is to blame.

4) Confess your anger to God and ask Him to forgive you for your response.

5) As far as it depends upon you, be at peace with all people.

6) Do something good for the person who was the target of your anger.

Start practicing living as a giver and not a taker. Choose to give a compliment, an encouraging word, a smile, or a small gift to someone today.

Choose to speak words that edify today. Before you speak, ask yourself—Is it true? Is it necessary? Will it encourage the hearer?

Well2Serve

CHAPTER 12

Focal Texts: Philippians 2:5–11; 2 Corinthians 9:6–15

Total fitness is no easy task! It requires serious commitment and continual discipline—which I'm sure you've realized from your long history of New Year's resolutions and your many attempts at turning over new leaves. You may have failed at so many other plans for a life-style change that you are skeptical about trying anything else. But before you decide the ideas in this book, while interesting, are too demanding or perhaps irrelevant to your life, consider this . . .

The principles we have been discussing are biblical prescriptions for wholeness, and therefore cannot be taken lightly or ignored. The care and maintenance of our bodies—the earthly dwelling place of the Spirit—is a biblical mandate. To disobey them, therefore, is sin. So these ideas are much more than the hyped up, feel-better claims of a fad diet or a temporary workout program. There's a much larger reason why the principles we've addressed should lead to a radical new life-style.

In one sense, this book is about you, because it will improve your all-around experience of life. But in a larger sense, it is not about you, because your purpose on earth is to advance God's kingdom by His power and for His glory. So more than anything, it is about Him. It's about delighting your Maker with the completely surrendered offering of yourself—every inch and ounce of it, inside and out. And when your chief reason for pursuing a total life make over is to fulfill His purpose for your life, you won't flame out at the first challenge to quit. Such a God centered motivation is more lasting than the self-centered motivation behind many wellness programs.

This is the kind of change you can finally do.

This is the kind of change you must do.

Created to Serve (Gen. 1:26–28)

We have now come full circle. We started by establishing the truth that we were created by God for His own purposes and glory. Man created in God's image is a rational, relational, and responsible being, and has been given the task of managing the entirety of creation by ruling over it and replenishing it.

Simply stated, man was created to be a steward of all that God created. And that includes us—the stewardship of our mind, body, and spirit.

We get confused because we often imagine that we are owners, but in truth God alone is the owner and we are His stewards. We enter this life with nothing we can claim credit for, nothing we can wield ownership over. And we will exit our life the same way. But when we understand that the Creator of all things chose us to manage His creation, we should be daily motivated to steward well the gifts He has given—our time, our talents, and all other earthly treasures.

But such a noble calling, so rich with opportunity, comes with great responsibility. Since we were created to serve God with our bodies, it stands to reason that we must present these bodies to Him as a living sacrifice (Rom. 12:1), for we will be held accountable for how we have used the resources given to us by God in

His service for His kingdom. And only in letting Him be the one to direct us and guide us will we be able to do our work well and use our bodies as He intended.

A Whole Body to Serve (Phil. 2:1–4)

Throughout our study, we have focused on the importance of the mind in adopting a life-style of wholeness. But for the Christian, it is not simply a matter of replacing negative thoughts with positive ones; it is a matter of replacing self-centered thoughts with Christ centered ones.

Paul, in trying to illustrate how the mind of the follower of Christ is distinguished from that of the unbeliever, uses a hymn which may have already been a part of the liturgy of the early church. The immediate context (Phil. 2:1–4) speaks of attitudes and actions which are essential to Christian community. We were not only created for service to the King; this service is to be expressed through His body, His earthly kingdom community—the church. Thus Paul precedes the presentation of the hymn on the mind of Christ with three distinctives that both define the nature of the believer and gauge the health of the church.

1. Paul calls the Philippians to a common outlook. He expresses this idea in several different ways— "being of the same mind, maintaining the same love, united in spirit, intent on one purpose" (v. 2). In order for a community made up of diverse members to have a shared mind-set, each person must value God's kingdom over his own kingdom. Do you live daily with kingdom focus? Is your purpose in life to advance God's kingdom by His power and for His glory?

135

2. Believers are called to radical humility. "Do nothing from selfishness or empty conceit, but with humility of mind regard one another as more important than yourselves" (v. 3). The Philippians were to avoid any behavior motivated by selfishness or vain conceit. When we act out of selfishness, we seek our own glory rather than God's glory. Selfishness must be replaced with humility, with an others oriented mentality.

Humility, however, had a quite negative connotation in the ancient world. The adjective related to it "was frequently employed, and especially so, to describe the mentality of a slave. It conveyed the ideas of being base, unfit, shabby, mean, of no account."[13] But in Christ, humility has been redefined and given royal status. That's why it is a major theme of the entire New Testament and remains a mandate for all who follow Christ.

3. Believers are givers, not consumers. To regard others as more important than ourselves does not mean we ignore our own concerns, as verse 4 makes clear. But Christians take care of even their own affairs as an act of love for other members of the body (1 Thess. 4:9–12). Any concern of one member of the body of Christ becomes the concern of every member of the body. You cannot read the book of Acts without recognizing that the early church definitely looked out for the welfare of their brothers and sisters (Acts 2:43–47; 4:32–35). In the same way, the reason we desire total wellness today is not motivated alone by concern for our own benefit. Our desire for being healthy is so

[13] Quotation from Hawthorne, *Philippians, 70, but cited from* Richard R. Melick, Jr. *Philippians Colossians Philemon in The New American Commentary* (Nashville: Broadman Press, 1991), p. 94.

that we can be *Well2Serve* others. Those who "live to give" are able to experience greater joy and fulfillment and thus have an overall healthier life-style.

How's that for another driving motivation to keep yourself healthy and strong? It's not just about you. Others are counting on you.

The Mind to Serve (Phil. 2:5–11)

Obviously, as we study Philippians 2:5–11, we cannot imitate some of the actions of Christ. We did not exist in the very form of God, for instance, and thus cannot lay aside deity nor take up humanity in the same manner Christ did. Nonetheless, we cannot ignore that Paul begins this section with a command—"Have this attitude in yourselves which was also in Christ Jesus" (v. 5). Paul insists that the believer must pattern his thinking on the model which Christ exhibited in the incarnation that led to His crucifixion. Throughout the hymn we find that Christ's attitude was evidenced by a concrete action. Thus we are to imitate His attitude which will, in turn, produce visible actions in our lives.

1. Jesus surrendered His rights by emptying Himself. The limited space in this book prevents us from exploring many of the profound truths about Jesus that occupy this early hymn—including, for example, the affirmation of His preexistence and His full deity. What a gloriously powerful truth of Scripture! Jesus is eternally and completely God! But for our purposes, we will focus on the attitudes we are instructed to embody as we learn to imitate Christ in our service.

This hymn tells us to consider the preexistent state

of Christ: He "existed in the form of God" (v. 6). The word "form" means an outward appearance consistent with what is true. The form perfectly expresses the inner reality.[14] The phrase "equality with God" is another way of saying that He exists originally and eternally as God. We don't possess the brain power to wrap our minds completely around this concept. And yet, understanding it as well as we can, we marvel at Jesus' attitude of surrender, that He "did not regard equality with God a thing to be grasped." The word translated "grasped" is not to be understood in the sense of grabbing what was not already His, but rather clinging to that which He already possessed. Jesus did not regard "equality with God" as a right or privilege to be used for His own advantage. Amazing!

This attitude of total surrender is what led Him to empty Himself of His position, rank, and privilege, making them of no effect during His earthly existence. The result of this emptying was that God became man. The Lord of lords became the servant of all. The eternal, sinless Christ became the sin offering for man. "Taking the form of a bond-servant" speaks of the attitude which produced the action of "being made in the likeness of man." Jesus cast aside His royal robes and donned human flesh.

Richard Melick, Jr. writes, "Jesus added servanthood to lordship as he added humanity to deity. In so doing he elevated humanity beyond what it had known before."[15] We could add that Christ elevated servanthood beyond what it had ever known before.

---

[14] Melick, p. 101.
[15] Ibid, p. 104.

Do you find that you often want to use your privilege and position for your own advantage rather than voluntarily emptying yourself for the good of others? Do you desire earthly success so that you can enjoy its benefits, or do you desire the means and opportunities to bless others? Even in desiring better health, are you thinking selfishly about how you want to look and feel, or are you seeing it as a selfless sacrifice for others?

2. Jesus humbled Himself by choosing radical obedience. When Jesus was "found in appearance as a man," he chose humility. His attitude of humility led to radical obedience which ultimately led to His death on the cross. He chose to obey even when obedience cost His life.

And His was no ordinary death. "Death on a cross" was the most ignoble way of all to die. No Roman citizen was allowed to be subjected to such a cruel form of death, yet the True Citizen of Heaven chose it as an act of obedience. The Jews saw it as a sign that the victim was cursed (Gal. 3:13), but Jesus saw it as the only solution to the curse of sin. The cross, so admired by Christians today, was a reproach and embarrassment to many in Jesus' day.

No one knows where radical obedience will lead or what it will require, but one thing is certain: it is our calling as followers and imitators of Christ. It will produce in us fullness of life, and will produce for us an eternal reward. In what areas are you sensing God calling you to total obedience where you've only given Him partial obedience before?

3. God rewards the life of surrendered servanthood. Verse 9 begins a transition in this passage where God

becomes the subject rather than Christ. Two of His actions show us His plan and pleasure: a) He exalted Christ and b) He gave Him a name above every name. Being exalted to the "highest" is quite a contrast with the lowliness represented by death on a cross. The name which is above every name is the title "Lord." Most commentators agree that this title refers to both His character and His function. By virtue of His surrender and obedience, He has now become the object of adoration in the Godhead and the administrator of all divine affairs.

Ultimately every knee of every creature—including spiritual beings both good and evil in the heavens, as well as all people living on earth and those already dead (under the earth)—will bow to Him. The language is that of triumph. Bending the knee is an act of submission to the one True Lord. This verse does not teach universal salvation, but rather the universal dominion of Christ over all creation.

The main principle we need to learn here is to desire God's praise rather than that of man. We get so caught up in worldly fame and fortune, we can neglect our created purpose: serving the King as we serve persons created in His image. But in His own time and purpose, God will exalt all who serve Him, even if for the time being it may not always appear so. Are you motivated more by the applause of man or the reward of God?[16]

---

[16] If you desire to study further on how to live for God's reward and thus lay up treasure in heaven, you would enjoy *Live it Up* by Ken Hemphill. It is available from Auxanopress.com.

Choose to Live Large (2 Cor. 9:6–15)

Most people live below their potential, afraid they don't have the ability or resources to make an impact. They live as if their life doesn't count. As a result, they live small—an impoverished life-style that does not indicate pious humility but rather a blatant disregard for their created purpose and the resources provided to them by the Creator of the Universe.

When our family moved to Virginia Beach, we purchased a home with a postage stamp sized yard. I had always dreamed of a lush green lawn, but because I was too cheap to buy a large bag of seed, I sprinkled seed sparingly. My lawn looked like a balding man with a bad comb over. My dad told me that seed was relatively inexpensive and should be used liberally. What a difference when I finally began sowing with generosity and abundance.

The apostle Paul also uses an agricultural image to encourage the Corinthians to live large. He is motivating them to join with other churches to provide an offering for the relief of the saints in Jerusalem who have been devastated by a famine. While the specifics of this chapter relate to money, the principles apply to every area of life.

Following is what I call the Four Laws of Large Living.

1. All else being equal, the quantity of the harvest will be proportionate to the quantity of the seed sown. This same principle is taught with slightly different images by the writer of Proverbs. "One person gives freely, yet gains more; another withholds what is right, only to become poor" (11:24 hcsb). "Kindness is a loan

to the Lord, and He will give a reward to the lender" (19:17 hcsb). This is the essence of Jesus' teaching as recorded in Luke 6:38—"Give, and it will be given to you. They will pour into your lap a good measure—pressed down, shaken together, and running over. For by your standard of measure, it will be measured to you in return." The first law of large living is to sow bountifully. Instead of addressing life with an attitude that says, "How little can I do and get by?" begin to think instead, "How much can I give?"

2. Sow cheerfully. Paul indicates that all genuine giving comes from the heart. It must emerge from an inner conviction that says giving always exceeds taking. When one gives "grudgingly" or "under compulsion," this indicates he is unwilling to part with what he considers to be his own. Further, it may indicate that he doesn't feel he possesses adequate resources to live large, and thus he begrudges the loss of anything that does not go directly to the meeting of his own needs and wants. Paul affirms that "God loves a cheerful giver" (v. 7). The word "loves" means "approves" or "rewards." This doesn't suggest that God doesn't love us when we fail to give; God loved us while we were yet sinners. The point is that God is a giver, and He loves to see His children reflect His character. When we choose to live large, we are living like God, and this brings Him joy.

3. Sow dependently. Too many Christians live as if their spiritual resources might run out. They fail to volunteer because they don't have the time. They refuse to forgive, thinking they just aren't able to do it. They give sparingly, afraid they might not have enough left

over for their own needs. All small living is based on a fundamental mistrust of God's resources made available to us for living. Listen carefully—"God is able to make all grace abound to you, so that always having all sufficiency in everything, you may have an abundance for every good deed" (v. 8). Did you notice these words—"all, always, everything, every"? The law of dependency could also be called the law of sufficiency. It is not simply related to giving but to living. This law is simple—when you have the desire to serve or give, God will always make it possible to do so out of His own generosity.

4. Trust in the law of multiplication. This fourth law is introduced and supported by a quotation from Psalm 112. In looking at the traits of the righteous, the psalmist declared: "How blessed is the man who fears the Lord, who greatly delights in His commandments" (v. 1). "Wealth and riches are in his house, and his righteousness endures forever" (v. 3). This happy man lends generously and conducts business fairly (v. 5). But it is the first part of verse 9 to which Paul pays particular attention: "He has given freely to the poor, his righteousness endures forever."

Paul declares three things God has promised to do for His people—a) He will provide seed for the sower and bread for food, b) He will multiply their seed, and c) He will increase the harvest of their righteousness. Notice that the promise includes enough for our needs (bread for food), but also additional resources for sowing into the lives of others. As if the provision of food and seed were not enough, God promises to multiply our quantity for sowing, challenging us to empty our bag of seed and trust Him to refill it. But it gets even better! God promises a fruitful harvest of righteousness. To have an abundance of seed is good; to know for certain that it will spring into life is pure joy.

Can you imagine the impact your life could achieve if you took God's promises seriously? Would you dare to live, serve, and give more freely, knowing that God will undoubtedly supply and multiply your seed for sowing?

The Four Results of Large Living

What happens when we choose to live large?

1. We become the recipients of our own generosity. "You will be enriched in everything for all liberality" (v. 11). Being "enriched in everything" is not for our benefit alone. God intends our generosity to give us freedom in every situation of life—with "all liberality." He enables us to continue to live large as we sow into the lives of others.

2. Living large enables us to supply people's needs. Paul refers to the offering for the saints in Jerusalem as a "ministry of service" (v. 12). This phrase brings together two theologically charged words. The first is diakonia, which means "service" and the other is leitergeio, which means "ritual or cultic service." Perhaps in reading these, you hear the English words "deacon" and "liturgy." In other words, service is an act of worship. You were created to serve. And when you do, your act of worship is well pleasing to God.

3. Living large produces thanksgiving to God. This theme dominates Paul's thinking in this section, and he repeats the emphasis three times. In Romans 1:21, Paul

indicates that unbelievers enjoy the benefits of God, but they do not glorify Him or show gratitude. They do not understand that everything they call their own actually comes from God, and thus they fail to live with a grateful heart.

In our present passage, the seed that was sown was seed that God provided. And this seed became the instrument through which God extended and demonstrated His grace to the saints in Jerusalem, which overflowed in many thanksgivings to God (v. 12). So you could say that living large creates a double dose of thanksgiving. First the Corinthians expressed thanksgiving through their generosity, and then the recipients of the gift thanked God, producing a swell of gratitude on both ends of the equation.

4. Living large glorifies God. Paul indicates that the recipients of the gift will "glorify God for your obedience" (v. 13). The sole end of man is to glorify God. When we choose to live large by sowing into the lives of others, we fulfill our created purpose. Does your lifestyle reflect the grace you have received? Does your giving of yourself in service adequately thank God for what He has done for you? Does your giving cause others to glorify God for your generosity?

This is what it means to be *Well2Serve*.

For Memory and Meditation
"Have this attitude in yourselves which also was in Christ Jesus" (Phil. 2:5).

WELL*FACTS*

I don't know what your destiny will be, but this I know: the only ones among you who will be truly happy are those who will have sought and found how to serve. Albert Schewitzer

The remarkable bottom line of the science of love is that giving protects overall health twice as much as aspirin protects against heart disease. Post, 7

But the remarkably good news is that, over the past ten years, we have about five hundred serious scientific studies that demonstrate the power of unselfish love to enhance health…. Post, 8

Giving in high school predicts good physical and mental health all the way into late adulthood, a time interval of over fifty years. Post, 8

A new study from Doug Oman of the University of California at Berkeley has followed almost two thousand individuals over fifty-five for five years. Those who volunteer for two or more organizations have an impressive 44 percent lower likelihood of dying—and that's after sifting out every other contributing factor, including physical health, exercise, gender, habits like smoking, marital status, and much more. Post, 8.

Gratification comes from the pursuit of something that you believe has meaning and value….What gives you a feeling of fulfillment—a sense that you have done something good for others? Find an outlet for your natural gifts and talents and then give yourself away to others. Colbert, 191.

WELL*ACTS*

Stephen Post and Jill Neimark indicate that there are four domains for loving service—family, friends, community, and humanity at large. As you think about acts of service, be sure to think in all four domains.

Post and Neimark speak of serving in many little ways. They suggest 10 ways of serving. These are included to stimulate your thinking. Celebration, generativity (nurturing others), forgiveness, courage (confrontation tempered by caring), humor, respect, compassion, loyalty, listening, and creativity. Think of ways of serving in each domain in one or more ways each day this week.

Volunteer for one service event this week. If you have a family, consider a family event that would include everyone, whatever their age.

Ask God to show you the most productive way you could serve your church or community, and seek training to begin serving there in a prolonged fashion.

Look for opportunities to give beyond the tithe. The tithe is the 10% that we return to the Lord through our church each week. Gifts beyond the tithe allow you to use spontaneous discretion in your extra giving.

Ask God to sensitize you to people who need an act of kindness, whether it is a smile, an encouraging word, or a friendly and appropriate touch. Look for one such opportunity every day this week.

Bibliography and Abbreviations for Well*Facts*

Daniel **Amen**, *The Amen Solution: The Brain Healthy Way to Lose Weight and Keep It Off*. eBook

Don **Colbert**, *Deadly Emotions*, (Nashville: Thomas Nelson Publishers, 2003).

Eric A **Finkelstein** and Laurie Zuckerman, *The Fattening of America: How the Economy Makes Us Fat, If it Matters, and What to Do about It*, eBook.

Daniel **Goleman**, *Emotional Intelligence: 10th Anniversary Edition*, eBook.

Rupert A **Hayles**, Jr. *Emotional Intelligence and the Church*, (Florida, Bridge Logos, 2010).

Carl **Honore** (2009-04-02). *In Praise of Slowness (Plus)* HarperOne. Kindle Edition.

Mark **Hyman**, *The Blood Sugar Solution*, (New York: Little, Brown and Company, 2012).

Kevin **Leman**, *Stopping Stress before It Stops You: A Game Plan for Every Mom*, eBook.

Jordan **Metzl** and Andrew Heffernan, *The Exercise Cure: A Doctor's All-Natural, No-Pill Prescription for Better Health and Longer Life*, eBook

Dean **Ornish**. *The Spectrum: How to Customize a Way of Eating and Living Just Right for You and Your Family*. eBook

Alice **Park**, *"Why Going to Church Can Make You Fat,"* Time Health and Family, March 24, 2011. http://healthland.time.com/2011/03/24/why-going-to-church-can-make-you-fat/

Stephen **Post** and Jill Neimark, *Why Good Things Happen to Good People,* (New York: Broadway Books, 2007)

Tom **Rath**, *Eat Move Sleep: How Small Choices Lead to Big Changes.* eBook

Steve **Reynolds**, *Bod 4 God: The Four Keys to Weight Loss.* eBook

Michael F. **Roizen** and Mehmet C. Oz, *You Staying Young,* (New York: Free Press, 2007).

Gretchen **Rubin**. *The Happiness Project: Or, Why I Spent a Year Trying to Sing in the Morning, Clean My Closets, Fight Right, Read Aristotle, and Generally Have More Fun,* eBook.

Hal **Urban**, *Life's Greatest Lessons: 20 Things That Matter,* (Fireside: Simon & Schuster, 2003)

Rick **Warren**, Daniel Amen, and Mark Hyman, *The Daniel Plan Study Guide: 40 Days to a Healthier Life,* eBook

The *Well2Serve* Statement of Belief

I believe...

I was created by God with **purpose**

Strong relationships are a key to life

The **foods and beverages** I put in my body impact my health and wellbeing

My body was made to **move**; by increasing my movement, my health will be significantly impacted

Good **rest** is essential to performing my best and fulfilling my responsibilities

Laughter with others is essential to wellbeing

Thankfulness is a characteristic of a believer and important to wellbeing

Forgiveness is a key component to my wellbeing

I can live my life so that I can **impact** those around me

Serving God and others gives **purpose** to my life and promotes wellness.

The *Well2serve* Call to Action

I will. . .

Live my life with **purpose and direction** and help others do the same

Choose to eat **real food** and **drink water** to nourish and provide health and healing to my body

Increase and **cherish time** spent with my spouse, children, friends, and other loved ones

Move my body daily and encourage others to do the same

Rest in order to perform to the best of my ability

Wake up **optimistic and enthusiastic** about the day ahead, never losing my sense of humor or adventure

Show **gratitude** toward and appreciation for those around me

Support and **encourage my teammates** because we are winning the game of life together

Seek to **serve others** in my community and beyond

Learn to easily and graciously **forgive** the wrongs of others

I pledge to do my very best to **encourage** those around me toward a place of wellness, supporting them and helping them in any way that I can.

Signed_____

To form your *Well2Win* team, go to www.Well2Win.com to register, create your team, and track your progress toward wellness.

Appendix A

The promises of this book are based on one's relationship to Christ. If you have not yet entered a personal relationship with Jesus Christ, I encourage you to make this wonderful discovery today. I like to use the very simple acrostic—LIFE—to explain this, knowing that God wants you not only to inherit *eternal* life but also to experience *earthly* life to its fullest.

L = Love

It all begins with God's Love. God created you in his image. This means you were created to live in relationship with him. *"For God loved the world in this way: He gave His One and Only Son, so that everyone who believes in Him will Not perish but have eternal life"* (John 3:16).

But if God loves you and desires a relationship with you, why do you feel so isolated from Him?

I = Isolation

This isolation is created by our sin—our rebellion against God—which separates us from him and from others. *"For all have sinned and fall short of the glory of God"* (Romans 3:23). *"For the wages of sin is death, but the gift of God is eternal life in Christ Jesus our Lord"* (Romans 6:23).

You might wonder how you can overcome this isolation and have an intimate relationship with God.

F = Forgiveness

The only solution to man's isolation and separation from a holy God is forgiveness. *"For Christ also suffered for sins once and for all, the righteous for the unrighteous, that He might bring you to God, after being put to death in the fleshly realm but made alive in the spiritual realm"* (1 Peter 3:18).

The only way our relationship can be restored with God is through the forgiveness of our sins. Jesus Christ died on the cross for this very purpose.

E = Eternal Life

You can have a full and abundant life in this present life... and eternal life when you die. *"But to all who did receive Him, He gave them the right to be children of God, to those who believe His name"* (John 1:12). *"A thief comes only to steal and to kill and to destroy. I have come that they may have life and have it in abundance"* (John 10:10).

Is there any reason you wouldn't like to have a personal relationship with God?

THE PLAN OF SALVATION

It's as simple as ABC. All you have to do is:

A = Admit you are a sinner. Turn from your sin and turn to God. *"Repent and turn back, that your sins may be wiped out so that seasons of refreshing may come from the presence of the Lord"* (Acts 3:19).

B = Believe that Jesus died for your sins and rose from the dead enabling you to have life. *"I have written these things to you who believe in the name of the Son of God, so that you may know that you have eternal life"* (1 John 5:13).

C = Confess verbally and publicly your belief in Jesus Christ. *"If you confess with your mouth, 'Jesus is Lord,' and believe in your heart that God raised Him from the dead, you will be saved. With the heart one believes, resulting in righteousness, and with the mouth one confesses, resulting in salvation"* (Rom. 10:9–10).

You can invite Jesus Christ to come into your life right now. Pray something like this:

"God, I admit that I am a sinner. I believe that you sent Jesus, who died on the cross and rose from the dead, paying the penalty for my sins. I am asking that you forgive me of my sin, and I receive your gift of eternal life. It is in Jesus' name that I ask for this gift. Amen."

Signed _____

Date _____

If you have a friend or family member who is a Christian, tell them about your decision. Then find a church that teaches the Bible, and let them help you go deeper with Christ.

Want to learn more about becoming Well2Serve?

Need fitness tips, recipes, family activity ideas?

Join our online community of people who are *Well2Win* and *Well2Serve* at www.Well2Win.com.

Free resources: exercises, education, recipes, quizzes, and more.

Or raise the bar and GET IN THE GAME. Once registered you will have access to: track you activity,

Join the *Well2Win* family of people just like you who desire to maximize their wellness in order to serve those around them. Get started today in three easy steps:

Go to www.Well2Win.com

Register as a New Team Leader

Form your own team to compete with other teams to earn points for prizes

Sign up and get started on your new wellness journey today!

Non-Disposable Curriculum

- Study the Bible and build a Christian library!
- Designed for use in any small group.
- Affordable, biblically based, and life oriented.
- Free teaching helps and administrative materials online.
- Choose your own material and stop/start time.

Audio-commentary material for teachers by the author at additional cost.

Other Volumes Available Now

Core Convictions: Confidence About What You Believe
When people have confidence about what they believe, they are more inclined to make daily decisions from a Biblical perspective. Ken Hemphill

Connected Community: Becoming Family Through Church
Only the church can deliver authentic community that will last forever. This study explores the mystery of God's eternal plan to reveal His manifold wisdom through the Church. Ken Hemphill

God's Redemption Story: Old Testament Survey
Explores the story line of the Old Testament by focusing on twelve key events in the life of Israel and linking them together to provide a unified view of God's redemptive work in history. Ken Hemphill

The King and His Community: New Testament Survey
Begins with the birth of Jesus and ends with Him walking among the seven churches of the book of Revelation. It covers key passages that tell the story of the King and the worldwide spread of His church. Kie Bowman

Pray Like It Matters: Intimacy And Power Through Prayer
Prayer makes a difference and it really matters and changes things in our lives as well as others. Our lack of spiritual power is due to our lack of prayer. God will use prayer to shake us and shape us. May He shape each of us into people who genuinely believe that prayer will draw us closer to Him and make us stronger in our faith. Steve Gaines, Ph.D.

Every Spiritual Blessing: A Study Of Ephesians
Ephesians contains some of the richest theology and practical teaching in all of the Bible, it is profound and challenging. As you study Ephesians, I pray you will embrace and express all the scriptual blessings made available to you in Christ. Ken Hemphill

For Teaching Helps
and Additional
Small Group Study
Materials Visit:
Auxanopress.com